Eating Korean in America

**FOOD
IN ASIA
AND THE
PACIFIC**

Series Editors:

Christine R. Yano and Robert Ji-Song Ku

Eating Korean in America

GASTRONOMIC ETHNOGRAPHY OF AUTHENTICITY

Sonia Ryang

University of Hawai'i Press | Honolulu

© 2015 University of Hawai'i Press
All rights reserved
Paperback edition 2016
Printed in the United States of America

21   20   19   18   17   16   6   5   4   3   2   1

Library of Congress Cataloging-in-Publication Data
Ryang, Sonia, author.
  Eating Korean in America : gastronomic ethnography of authenticity /
Sonia Ryang.
        pages cm — (Food in Asia and the Pacific)
  Includes bibliographical references and index.
  ISBN 978-0-8248-3935-2 (cloth : alk. paper)
  1. Cooking, Korean.   2. Food habits—United States.   I. Title.
II. Series: Food in Asia and the Pacific.
  TX724.5.K65R93 2015
  641.59519—dc23
                                                              2014037414

ISBN 978-0-8248-5343-3 (pbk. : alk. paper)

University of Hawai'i Press books are printed on acid-free
paper and meet the guidelines for permanence and durability
of the Council on Library Resources.

Printed by Sheridan Books, Inc.

For Sid, in grateful appreciation for all the Thanksgiving meals
you invited me to—each one a true feast in all kinds of ways

Contents

Acknowledgments

This book came into being by accident. In the fall of 1997 I happened to land my first academic position at The Johns Hopkins University in Baltimore, thereby becoming a colleague of esteemed anthropologists whose work I had read and admired as a student. Of all these people, it was Sidney Mintz whose name lured me to Hopkins; I had marveled at his *Sweetness and Power* while studying social anthropology at Cambridge University. Many great and wonderful things flowed from my contact with Sid, one of them being the opportunity to sample his incredible cooking and benefit from his vast knowledge of food. He showed me when to eat what, and in what way. His dishes I had the honor of sampling consisted of commonplace ingredients masterfully combined to create exquisite flavors. There was his tarragon lamb, his wild-rice side dish, and lots of interesting soups—my mouth is watering just thinking about them.

Sid's generous approach to the enjoyment of food was an eye-opener to me. As I had been an international student from Japan in England and then a postdoctoral fellow in Australia, my personal life did not allow much time for enjoying good meals, let alone for cooking them myself. Sid taught me how one should appreciate life—namely, as a human being first and then as an academic. The stories he told me about food were funny and memorable yet always had an important message that taught me about aspects of human society. Since then, the Johns Hopkins anthropology department has changed considerably, with departures and new arrivals, and no longer does it even look the same, but the origin of this book can be traced to that department as it was in 1997. I wish to acknowledge that without Sidney Mintz this book would not have come into being.

As with all the other books I have written, my editor at the press played an important role in its completion. I would like to thank Masako Ikeda of the University of Hawai'i Press for her impeccable professionalism and extraordinary support for my work. Without Masako this book would not have come into being either. The manuscript has also benefited enormously from the constructive and insightful comments of two readers. In particular, the suggestion of one of them, Mari Yoshihara, that I take an extra look at Honolulu, Hawai'i, yielded an incredibly useful result, for which I am grateful. Other editorial personnel, Debra Tang in particular, and members of the production team at the press were extremely helpful, turning the experience of publishing with the University of Hawai'i Press pleasant and memorable.

While gathering ethnographic data, many people helped me write the book by eating Korean food with me. At the University of Iowa I would like to extend particular gratitude to my research assistant, Whitney Brewer, an undergraduate student when she worked for me, who braved the journey to Los Angeles' Koreatown and tasted Korean food over a number of weeks in order to compile a report for me. Whitney's travel was funded by the Iowa Center for Research by Undergraduates (ICRU) initiative, the assistance of which I gratefully acknowledge here. In addition to Whitney, many of my friends, colleagues, and students kept me company in my eating endeavors, providing me with valuable insights in relation to their gastronomic experiences. My copy editor, Donald Cameron, has done another remarkable job turning my book into a better, superior form.

The research for this book was generously funded by the Academy of Korean Studies (Competitive Research Grant AKS-2011-R 59 Global Hansik: Korean Food in the U.S., 2010–2011; AKS-2912–10R59, 2011–2012). I thank the funding agency for its support. The College of Liberal Arts and Sciences and the Department of Anthropology at the University of Iowa kindly agreed to adjust my teaching schedule in order to make time for me to write. Many of my colleagues at the University of Iowa were active interlocutors throughout the research, which helped me sustain my focus and curiosity. Without the intellectual environment that I have enjoyed on the Iowa campus, I would not have been able to complete this research in such an enjoyable and fulfilling manner.

All photos in this volume are taken by me and collated in the color plates section. Readers are asked to refer to this section when items appearing in these photos are described in the text. I wish to thank the University of Iowa for letting me allocate a portion of my research budget toward the production of color photos.

Studying the ways in which food is produced, distributed, and consumed offers a crucial key to understanding the socioeconomic fundamentals of our own society and those of other nations. Yet, the experience of eating remains such a personal thing, mostly embedded in the context of family life. At home, my family has a strange eating arrangement. We long ago abolished the ritual of the family dinner. Our daughter's severe disability means that she "eats" via a feeding tube inserted into her abdomen. She needs to be given a set formula every three hours during the day, while pump feeding sustains her nutritional needs during the night. In light of this, and in order not to make her feel excluded, we decided not to be rigid about the family dinner. My husband enjoys meat, most likely reflecting his upbringing in the Midwest, while my twelve-year-old son has peculiar dietary habits, eating only a few items on a regular basis. Indeed, it is a struggle to avoid giving him the kind of processed, artificial, and fattening food overly prevalent on the shelves of U.S. supermarkets today. However, my husband's liking for *kimchi* (especially cucumber *kimchi*) and my son's love for sticky Korean rice allow us to have some kind of Korean component in our meals. Despite all of these idiosyncratic peculiarities, without my family I would not have been able to think about food, let alone write this book. As always, they have been my bedrock in producing this work and have provided sustained support for my commitment.

As for myself, while writing this book, I discovered the pleasure of fasting. In the process of conducting this research, I came to realize how much we eat and how we eat much more than we need to. Consciously eating less or sometimes skipping meals made me realize how wastefully I eat without even thinking about the act of eating. Needless to say, I can state as such because I do not face the crisis of starvation. Millions of people in the world live with that reality every day; for them, not eating may well be the only option. I would like to stress that even though this book is about food and eating, it is my hope that it will be read with the understanding that a large portion of the humanity today does not have sufficient food to eat.

Introduction

Can Food Be Both National and Global?

When thinking about Korean food in the United States, a question immediately presents itself. Can a food still bear a national identity even after it has traveled beyond the boundaries of the nation in which it originated? This book attempts to explore some of the challenges prompted by this question, which at first appears innocuous but on closer examination reveals a contradiction.

At the outset, it is necessary to emphasize that the Korean food I will be introducing in this book may not be so Korean after all, as this will depend on how we define the national identity of particular foods. According to Sidney Mintz, the entire notion of "national cuisine" is a problematic one, as cuisines are by definition regional, not national (Mintz 2002). If we looked at the types of cuisine found within the boundaries of today's nation-states, we would likely discover that no nation had only one cuisine. However, as has been observed in many cases, government intervention can indeed make a certain cuisine "national" through claims of traditional ownership or authenticity in relation to such foods (e.g., Helstosky 2003; Lindholm 2008; Pérez and Abarca 2007). Indeed, in certain bizarre outbursts of nationalist fervor, governments have even been known to claim national ownership of a particular variety of cuisine by way of artificially standardizing it.

In recent times, the Korean government involved itself in such an endeavor in relation to *kimchi*. It is no secret that the Korean government and its people take considerable pride in *kimchi* as a unique and superior-quality fermented dish. For example, the director of the Institute of Traditional

1

Korean Food in Seoul makes the claim in a *kimchi* cookbook that the inclusion of this food in the daily diet of Koreans played a significant role in preventing them from contracting SARS (Severe Acute Respiratory Syndrome) when the epidemic broke out in 2002–2003, although the same author is silent in relation to the fact that Korea ranks among those countries with the highest incidence of gastric cancer (Hyun Ja Kim et al. 2002; Lee, Yang, and Ahn 2002; Yoon 2005).

In 1996, in response to Japanese commercial labeling of pickled vegetables as *kimuchi* (the Japanese pronunciation of this food) and Japan's attempt to include *kimuchi* as an official food for the Atlanta Olympic Games, the Korean government claimed that the Japanese product was not authentic—arguing, for example, that it had not been fermented ("Japan Korea" 2001). Korea lobbied for international standards to be applied to the production of *kimchi* by the Codex Alimentarius, an organization associated with the World Health Organization that defines voluntary standards in relation to food preparation for the purposes of international trade. A Codex Alimentarius ruling in 2001 described production methods similar to those traditionally used in Korea and unequivocally proscribed the product from being referred to as *kimuchi* rather than *kimchi*, in theory preventing Japan or any other nation from producing *kimchi* of its own (Codex Stan 2001). In 2009, the government-run Korea Food Research Institute went even further, standardizing Korean food recipes on a national level and claiming the intellectual property rights for them. This was a most curious strategy: Nowhere in Korea has *kimchi* been standardized or patented by any particular company or producer. Different types of *kimchi* require different degrees of fermentation, ranging from very short periods to durations of several months, for example. On a visit to a high-end supermarket attached to an exquisite department store in Seoul in 2009, I found no fewer than six different counters selling various kinds of freshly prepared napa cabbage and other types of *kimchi* in addition to a chilled food section offering twelve different brands of packaged *kimchi* and eight different kinds of ready-mixed packets of spices for making *kimchi*.

Despite attempts by the Korean government to standardize *kimchi* as a form of national culinary property, most Koreans themselves would have a hard time imagining, let alone producing, a nationally standardized version of this food. This is because the way in which *kimchi* is produced varies from region to region and from family to family. The *kimchi* question becomes even more anomalous if we think about how it is produced and consumed in the United States. Even on the shelves of conventional supermarkets, it is possible to find jars of *kimchi* bearing Chinese brand names and marked "Product of USA." Others, such as Sunja's *kimchee,* have Korean-sounding names (Sunja being a Korean female name) while being marked as having been produced in the United States. According to my testing, some appear not to have been fermented but instead mixed with spicy sauce, while others appear to be have been properly fermented, the contents at times even bubbling over the top of the jar when newly opened. Where in this picture can we find the standardized form of *kimchi* that the Korean government claims as exclusive national property?

This question aside, not many people would disagree with the claim that *kimchi* is, in a most unequivocal way, Korean. When unseasonable weather led to a cabbage shortage early in 2010, the government stepped in by bailing out *kimchi* producers in order to satisfy the national "need" (so to speak) to such an extent that it became international news ("Cabbage Shortage" 2010; Gliona 2010; Jeanne Park 2010). Against such a background, one might ask: How can a food be both national and global at the same time? Clearly, recent actions taken by the Korean government have been driven by a desire to delineate the boundaries of the nation's culinary property on the global stage. Yet such tactics may not only lead to the risk of national authenticity being compromised whenever others create their own versions of that particular cuisine, but also create obstacles to the advancement of the national cuisine within the global market.

The irony is that food is not thought of or classified in nationally standardized ways in Korea itself; on the contrary, the existence of regionally diverse cuisines is a source of excitement for consumers. Furthermore, Koreans do not eat only Korean food, also enjoying various types of ethnic cuisine from different parts of the world, in addition to so-called fusion food, at a wide variety of establishments—from inexpensive local eateries all the way up to haute cuisine restaurants. *Wesik saneop* (literally, "the eating-out industry") is now so competitive in Korea that one often comes across claims on television that a particular restaurant is the guardian of secret recipes passed down from generation to generation that allow it to prepare certain dishes in ways that others are unable to replicate. Thus, rather than becoming more and more standardized, food in Korea is actually diversifying in an ever more vigorous manner.

By contrast, once outside Korean national boundaries, Korean food finds itself associated with national identity and authenticity rather than with particular regions or secret multigenerational family recipes. Thus, even though their chefs may come from different parts of Korea or not from Korea at all, Korean restaurants in the United States serve something known as "Korean" food—in so doing invoking, in a sense, an association with what may be termed Korea's national authenticity. The fact that each restaurant uses different recipes (many of which may well be secret) does not diminish that restaurant's status as Korean. It would seem, therefore, that once outside of its national boundaries, the regional identity of a particular food is quickly replaced by a national identity.

Sidney Mintz argues that Americans do not have their own national cuisine (Mintz 2002). I can concur, given the absence of "American restaurants" in Europe or Asia, for example. Whereas in Seoul I came across Japanese, Italian, Chinese, French, Thai, Indian, Indonesian, Malaysian, Nepalese, Ethiopian, Greek, and Turkish restaurants, I encountered no American restaurants other than franchise establishments such as McDonald's, KFC, and Burger King. Yet, as many existing studies have shown, even chains like McDonald's adapt themselves to the local palate as they expand in foreign markets—for instance, the company's Beijing outlet serves a rice dish (Watson 2005). At the same time, it has become increasingly common to encounter the term "American" on the restaurant scene inside the United States itself, even though I have yet to grasp what this means. In Iowa City, one of my fieldwork locations, restaurants calling themselves "American" include establishments that serve dishes such as "Pasta la Jolla," "Bruschetta," "Black Bean Hummus," and "Thai Chicken Burrito." What does this tell us about American food or food in the United States? By the same token, what does it tell us about food in Korea? And on what basis does Korean food in the United States and elsewhere claim to have national authenticity? Furthermore, what kind of authenticity are we talking about when discussing it in the context of food and the act of eating? These are the key questions considered in this book as we examine how four Korean dishes—*naengmyeon* (chilled noodle soup), *jeon* (pancakes), *galbi* (barbecued beef/short ribs), and *bibimbap* (a bowl of rice mixed with vegetables)—are presented and consumed at four different locations throughout the United States: Los Angeles, Baltimore, Hawai'i (Kona and Honolulu), and Iowa City.

Food in the United States

Thinking about Korean food in the United States requires that we first understand the food culture of the environment into which Korean food is being introduced. Historically, food and eating practices in the United States have displayed unique and highly unusual characteristics, at least from around the time of the Great Depression. Indeed, the United States can be clearly differentiated from nations in many other parts of the world, including Korea, in its abundance of food and enormous amount of waste and overconsumption. Anyone walking into a standard American supermarket would immediately marvel at the enormous volume of food items available. Americans have been and remain what we may call overeaters. European visitors to the United States in previous centuries were already commenting about wasteful patterns of food consumption and the way in which quality was sacrificed to quantity in the American diet. Based largely on a British and/or northwestern European diet, American meals were dominated by meat or, more precisely, beef, and displayed a distinct lack of fresh fruits and vegetables.

The late nineteenth and early twentieth centuries saw the rise of the food-processing industry in the United States. Familiar names such as Kellogg's and Nabisco (National Biscuit Company) originate from this period, which also witnessed the beginning of the mass production of canned and bottled foods. During this time, reformers and chemists devoted considerable attention to the cost of food for the working poor. Ventures such as the New England Kitchen (Levinstein 2003b: chap. 4) resulted from a desire to reduce the food bills of the working class without compromising its caloric intake—thereby improving labor output at lower cost. Vitamins and minerals were introduced into the American diet from the 1910s through the 1930s, while the disparity between a wasteful, overeating upper class and a poorly nourished working class persisted (Levinstein 2003b: chap.12). Even during World War II, U.S. soldiers were the best fed of the day. After the war had come to an end, the enormous quantity of food on the shelves of GI stores during the U.S. occupation of Japan (1945–1952), including giant cans of meat and vegetables, was the object of extreme envy among the near-starved Japanese.

Historians note that Americans have not been accustomed to the idea of food shortages (and the practices associated with such conditions). Even in times of crisis, such as during the Great Depression or in times of war, Americans have displayed a considerable amount of suspicion in response to official references to food shortages (Levinstein 2003a). Intuitively speaking, history seems to tell us that Americans, as a nation, have not experienced a crisis that involves the real-life threat of starvation. This is not, however, the case for every American. Indeed, there are two competing histories of food and eating in America: one for the rich and one for the poor. The rich have always consumed large quantities of food—more than they needed to—their diets including a quality mix of imported foreign produce as well as prime domestic produce. The poor, in contrast, have struggled to bridge the gap between their meager incomes and the high prices charged even for foods of inferior nutritive value. While infant mortality rates among members of the former group had improved by 1930, those of the latter group remained very high (Levinstein 2003a). Nevertheless, it should still be emphasized that a large number of Americans never experienced the conditions of near starvation encountered by many other peoples throughout the modern world.

By the time World War II ended, most parts of the world, including Europe, had experienced considerable food shortages. Much of Japan lay flattened, two of its cities destroyed by atom bombs, and many other parts of the world experienced further crises during the postwar years. The Korean Peninsula was devastated during the Korean War (1950–1953), napalm and Agent Orange destroyed Vietnamese lives, homes, and land during the 1960s, and severe famine in China during the Cultural Revolution of the late 1960s drastically reduced its population. By contrast, the United States as a whole remained in much better condition during these decades. Its economy grew exponentially during the postwar period, while its wealthy class became even wealthier by global standards. Up until the 1980s, even middle-class Americans enjoyed a good quality of life, owning their own homes and automobiles, enjoying annual vacations, and benefiting from access to affordable health care and retirement savings. In the process, eating (or overeating) became part of everyday culture in the United States from an early stage—and, most likely, much sooner than was the case in other nations such as Korea or Japan, which had to struggle to secure enough food to eat for their populations before being able to critically reflect on the subject.

As Americans began eating greater quantities of fast food and other foods with a high fat content, their body weights and the nation's health-care costs continued to rise. This development did not take place in a vacuum. Industrialized agriculture, corporate lobbying of the FDA (Food and Drug Administration) and other government offices and lawmakers, pharmaceutical interests, the nutritional supplement industry, and other key elements of the late-capitalist food industry all played a part. A focus on enhanced industrialization and profit maximization has made the U.S. food industry "top-heavy," with a staggering degree of monopolization among food suppliers. Already in 1987 the ten largest restaurant franchise businesses accounted for nearly 60 percent of the sales volume of the top one hundred, an example of the concentration of corporate profit in fewer hands (Levinstein 2003a: 247–248). In 2010, McDonald's controlled 15 percent of the U.S. fast-food market with more than 14,000 outlets, while also operating more than 31,000 restaurants in one hundred countries worldwide (Albritton 2009: 121; Hauter 2012: 67). As consumers struggled to reduce their food bills, there was an increase in levels of consumption of fast food and cheap TV dinners. Indeed, almost half of the people sampled in a Gallup poll in 1989 were sitting down to eat frozen, packaged, or take-out meals at home, "spending 15 percent of the national food dollar on these pizzas, chickens, and submarine sandwiches" (Levinstein 2003a: 249).

Indeed, fast and cheap are becoming the key terms to describe food consumption in America, the scene now dominated and dictated to by food corporations and industrialized agriculture. In 2012, the top four U.S. retailers—Walmart, Kroger, Costco, and Target—accounted for 50 percent of all grocery sales (Hauter 2012: 69). While it is true that recent decades have seen many Americans embrace organic and locally sourced food choices (such as those offered through food cooperatives or farmers' markets), going all-organic incurs substantially larger costs than following a diet based on conventional foods. When students in one of my anthropology classes conducted a food-related mini-research project in fall 2011, those focusing on organic food reached the unanimous conclusion that an exclusively organic diet was definitely beyond the means of average residents in Iowa City.

A similar picture of corporate domination can be found in the nutritional supplement and herbal product markets. The United States has a long tradition of incorporating vitamin and mineral products into regular diets. But efforts at deregulation pursued by recent administrations, notably the enactment of the Dietary Supplement Health and Education Act of 1994 (DSHEA), have had lasting effects. The new, altogether looser set of criteria for claiming health benefits, particularly as they relate to supplementary products, motivated food and drug companies to begin producing and marketing foods enhanced with supplements and over-the-counter medicines containing herbs and vitamins. By 1999, the value of supplement sales had increased from $4 billion to $15 billion, while sales of herbal supplements increased by 269 percent between 1996 and 1999, with sales of dietary supplements (including pills as well as foods with dietary supplements) predicted to surpass $30 billion by 2005 (Nestle 2007: 273). Thanks to the DSHEA, not only were food companies now able to market their products as dietary supplements and avoid the cumbersome approval process for new ingredients, drug companies were also now able to enter the food-as-supplement market by marketing foods as having therapeutic benefits without having to go through the drug approval process.

As a result, consumers now face a highly confusing situation when shopping for food. While presented with an unwieldy volume of food-related information, they are largely left in the dark when attempting to verify the potential benefits or harm that consumption of a particular food item will bring them. Marion Nestle neatly sums up the state of affairs in today's U.S. food market as follows: "The food industry uses lobbying, lawsuits, financial contributions, public relations, advertising, partnerships and alliances, philanthropy, threats, and biased information to convince Congress, federal agencies, nutrition and health professionals, and the public that the science relating diet to health is so confusing that they need not worry about diets: When it comes to diets, anything goes" (Nestle 2007: 358). Nestle, a well-known nutritionist, adds that the message that it is better for one's health to eat less is being systematically thwarted by an opposing message from the food industry encouraging people to eat more (Nestle 2007: 359). It is true that the U.S. food market possibly offers one of the largest varieties of food items available to consumers in the world—whether organic or conventional, sourced locally or from overseas. However, when we think about the conditions under which food items are made available to U.S. consumers, it is clear that so-called freedom of choice is nothing but a myth. This is because such freedom is fundamentally restricted by the way in which the food industry and large corporations control production and distribution on the one hand and by the limitations of our own financial means on the other, in an environment in which aggressive marketing, concealment of information, and avoidance of precise and comprehensive labeling is commonplace (Albritton 2009: 171–181).

The most acute feature of the current U.S. food environment is the alarmingly widening gap between rich and poor, a development in which those involved in policy implementation are complicit. The Global Financial Crisis hit the United States in 2008, following several years of economic expansion between 2000 and 2007, and it was revealed that while there had been an 18 percent growth in GDP during that period, poverty rates had also risen—from 11.3 percent to 12.5 percent. Statistics from 2010 showed that forty-nine million Americans, or 16.1 percent of the population, were struggling with hunger (Food Research and Action Center 2013: 13–14). Beginning in the 1960s, the U.S. government has set up federal programs to assist households experiencing food shortages. Through the Supplemental Nutrition Assistance Program (SNAP), formerly known as the Food Stamp Program, and other programs, $74.6 billion in food assistance was distributed in 2012, with 47.7 million Americans receiving, on average, $134.29 per month (SNAP Monthly Data 2013). November 2013 saw the termination of the temporary boost to SNAP benefits included in the 2009 American Recovery and Reinvestment Acts, leading to an average $36 reduction in the monthly food assistance provided to a four-person household (Dean and Rosenbaum 2013). This development will lead to increased hardship and food insecurity for millions of Americans in low-income families, many of whom are children.

Food in Korea

Many standard Korean cookbooks specializing in *hanguk eumsik* (Korean food) or *uri eumsik* (our food) contain paragraphs similar to the following example:

> In the palace, royal cuisine developed using all sorts of precious and rare ingredients sent from diverse parts of the nation, while locally, [Koreans] developed a rich variety of native foods using unique ingredients. If we were to summarize the characteristics of Korean food, which has its basis in [Korea's] natural, cultural, and social backgrounds, we would notice that Korean food is divided into [what might be termed] main food and supplemental food, based on the superior cooking method [known as] *yaksik dongwon* [a term meaning that medicine and food have the same origin], and that it is characterized by the development of the cooking of grains and fermented foods, such as *kimchi, jeotgal* [a thick base sauce or condiment mainly made

of raw fish or shellfish], and *jang* [sauce]. In addition, food preparation methods as well as table manners have followed Confucian teachings.

Our ancestors valued sincerity and harmony when preparing food. We prepare food with a straight posture and a clean [method]. The combination of taste and nutrition that Korean food carries today is the product of the scientific approach that [our ancestors] wisely developed eons ago. We must understand our characteristic food and continue developing Korea's traditional culinary culture. (Kim, Han, and Kim 2005: 10–11; author's translation)

The reader will have concluded that, as a whole, the above paragraph does not make sense. Aside from questioning the generalizations it contains, one also has to ask where it would be possible to find such a science of Korean food, or how one could ascertain whether or not Korean food was prepared using the right posture. Furthermore, one might ask oneself which ethnic food does not have its own sauce or pickled vegetables. At the very least, it is possible to conclude from the above quotation that commentaries on Korean food in Korea bear a strong tang of national pride.

It is true that food in Korea enjoys a unique and rich history, at least one that contrasts sharply with that of the United States. Whereas in the United States the destruction of native American culinary (and other) cultures, in addition to recurring waves of immigration, have led to the development of what commentators are ready to call "Americanized food," in Korea, Koreanization is not so much an issue. But precisely because it is taken for granted that Koreans do have their own unique culinary tradition, controversy can arise when market forces and intensifying competition in the fields of food production, distribution, and consumption lead to greater differentiation. Under such conditions, with what degree of certainty can we claim that there is such a thing as Korean food? Local diversity in cuisine as well as fusion or experimental recipes based on Korean cooking can be found in Korea today, just as they have existed in the past. However, given the fact that Korea has traditionally not had a history of accepting immigrants, there have been few opportunities for different cuisines to heavily influence Korean food, historically speaking.

On further examination, however, it is possible to conclude that Korean food has never been purely Korean. During the Goryeo dynasty (918–1392), Korea came under the strong influence of Buddhism, the religion adopted by the royal family. Thus, at least in theory, the killing of animals was forbidden. However, during the Mongol occupation of the thirteenth century,

Korean food came under Mongol influence, resulting in the development of a variety of dairy and meat-oriented dishes during the late Goryeo period (Young Jin Song 2010: 17). Under the Joseon dynasty (1392–1910), with the rejection of Buddhism and the embracing of Confucianism, meat became part of the regular diet—if one had the means to afford it, that is. Animals for slaughter included dogs, chicken, ducks, goats, and occasionally pigs. The meat of cows and horses was eaten more rarely due to the utility of these animals for farming. Meat was always used in a resourceful and economical way, with little waste. Tripe and organs, feet and heads, tails and eyes—all were eaten, one way or another (see Chapter 3).

By and large, however, traditional Korean food remained rich in plant-based food items. Vegetables and fruits, nuts and roots, sometimes even flowers, were important elements of the regular diet. And, needless to say, boiled rice (glutinous or sticky) was and still is the primary source of carbohydrates in the Korean diet, although noodles, prepared using various methods and incorporating a diverse range of local ingredients, were also consumed (see Chapter 1). The famed *kimchi* was already being enjoyed during the Goryeo dynasty, although red chili peppers, now perhaps the most crucial ingredient used in the production of *kimchi,* only reached Korea during the Japanese invasion at the end of the sixteenth century (Jo 2001). Matsuo Bashō, a famed poet of medieval Japan, made reference to chili peppers, native to South America, in several of his *haiku.* Before that time, *kimchi* in Korea was basically white or green. Often it did not even require fermentation, consisting of sliced or chopped vegetables soaked for a long time in a chilled broth mixed with salt and spices.

Traditionally speaking, Korean food played an important role in ritual and medicine. Even today, one can easily observe ingredients that in the West might be classified as herbal or medicinal, such as *jinseng (insam),* being used as regular components of well-established dishes like *samgyetang,* a soup dish consisting of a whole chicken stuffed with *jinseng* and *daechu* (dried dates; also known as jujubes). As early as the seventeenth century, Dutch traveler Hendrick Hamel recognized *jinseng* as an indigenous Korean food (Chun and Baek 2004: 10). Fruits and flowers have also long constituted important (if not nutritional) ingredients in the preparation of ritual foods. Azalea and chrysanthemum flowers were each used in spring and autumn feasts *(sisik),* while fruits and fruit juices were the main sources of marinades and other sauces for sweetening. Ritual food became a regular part of ordinary people's lives during the Joseon dynasty, a reflection of the regime's eager embrace of Confucianism. As such, ancestor commemoration rituals known as *jesa,* accompanied by their unique way of preparing food offerings (see Chapter 2), came to bear the utmost significance from the royal court right down to the commoner household.

Feasts that included prescribed and proscribed menu items were also prepared for other important events, such as weddings, funerals, *baegil* (the celebration of the one-hundredth day since the birth of a child), and the birthdays of senior family members, in addition to seasonal celebratory feasts, beginning with New Year's Day (Bok-jin Han 2009). Tables were set individually, each person having the entire course laid out right in front of him, divided up and presented in a series of small plates and bowls. The guest would be served three, five, or seven dishes, depending on his rank and relationship to the family (Choi et al. 2007: 26ff.). My use of the sexist words, him/his, here is intentional, as men usually sat at these tables, while women either served or prepared the food if the family had no servants. Thus, the sharing of large dishes was not part of Korean tradition—except in the case of the poor. The ironical fact is that, until recent times, most of the Korean population could not afford to enjoy such elaborate meals, with their multiple side dishes in addition to bowls of rice and soup, served on individually set tables. Indeed, for the majority of Koreans, simply securing enough to eat was the foremost concern through the dynastic, colonial, and postcolonial periods, and right up until very recent times.

During the Joseon dynasty (1392–1910), Korean society was characterized by a strict hierarchy according to which the population was divided into the following categories: the aristocracy, commoners, *jungin* (literally, "middle people," but best translated as artisans and craftsmen), and *nobi* (male and female slaves). The *jungin* and *nobi* were bound to their caste-like occupational roles. However, while the former were seen as fulfilling important and useful roles, the latter were seen as expendable. Commoners accounted for the bulk of the agricultural workforce. Even during periods when they did not have enough food to eat, the king continued to eat his five meals a day. Known as *surasang,* each of these meals included twenty-seven dishes, a bowl of red rice, a bowl of white rice, and soup, along with condiments and sauces. By default, these meals would include delicacies from around the country, from abalone taken from southern waters to boar meat from the northern mountains. Hundreds of court ladies, chefs, physicians, herbalists, and other workers, mostly consisting of court *nobi* as well as *jungin* with culinary, herbal, and medicinal skills, were mobilized to prepare the king's *surasang* (Bok-ryeo Han 2004: chap.1).

Under Japanese colonial rule (1910–1945), Koreans experienced considerable difficulties in relation to farming and food supply. Korean rice was routinely exported to Japan, while Koreans ate other foods, providing a typical example of a colonial agricultural structure where colonies supply crops to the colonial metropolis, leaving the colonized people without sufficient food. The land survey initiated by the Japanese during the early years of colonial rule unequivocally divided Koreans into two groups: a tiny number of landowners and a vast landless majority. During the colonial era, Korea was plagued by chronic malnutrition, food shortages, and a general struggle for survival. Soon after World War II, the peninsula was devastated by a civil war (1950–1953), which saw farmland destroyed and led to a further deterioration in the nation's ability to produce and supply food. Indeed, World Bank statistics show that Korea had an infant mortality rate of 82 per thousand births as recently as 1960. Until the 1970s, Korea was an agricultural nation. Since the 1970s, however, changes have occurred in the food market that reflect the nation's general economic growth, albeit under the control of heavy-handed military dictatorships. In the late 1980s, as the nation began to throw off the shackles of military rule and shift toward civilian government, and especially following aggressive deregulation in the aftermath of the 1997 IMF crisis—a severe market collapse that precipitated the bail-out of Korean economy by the International Monetary Fund—fundamentally new patterns of food supply and consumption began to emerge, notably, larger volume of food consumption, heavier dependence on imported foods, and a widening gap between rich overeaters and poor undereaters.

Obviously, Korea is richer and healthier now than it was in the past. World Bank statistics show that, by 2010, the nation's infant mortality rate had fallen to 4.16 per thousand live births. In 2005, the proportion of the national diet represented by animal products reached historically high levels (Hye-Kyung Park 2008: 343). Today, 90 percent of the Korean population lives in urban areas, which tend to have extremely high population densities. By contrast, there has been a process of depopulation in rural areas, the proportion of the population engaged in agriculture having dropped to a mere 5 percent (Ju 2000: S195). Furthermore, imports now make up more than 90 percent of Korea's food supply, including almost all of its corn and wheat. This state of affairs has even led the government to embark on the novel approach of buying farmland overseas in order to further ensure the nation's food security (Berthelsen 2011). There is also no doubt that South Koreans are eating more than before. While specialists note that Korea is relatively well placed in its consumption of fruit and vegetables, there has also been an increase in the proportion of adults who are overweight (23.5 percent of women and 24.3 percent of men in 1998), with an inverse relationship between obesity and levels of income and education (Lee, Popkin, and Kim 2002). Fast-food franchises and other American establishments are no less ubiquitous in Korea than in many other parts of the world. Not only are Koreans consuming greater quantities of animal products, their diets are tending to become increasingly fat-heavy. As a result, food producers in South Korea have eagerly embraced the catchall term *welbing*, derived from the English term well-being, while organic food and alternative cooking methods attract intense media attention (Young-Kyun Yang 2010: 85–87).

Recently, South Korea has seen a revival in the royal culinary arts, as portrayed in the popular television show *Daejanggeum* (2003, MBC), a period drama featuring a chef and herbalist in the royal court who eventually ascends to the rank of physician and chef to the king—these two offices having been merged during the Joseon dynasty under the principle of *yaksik dongwon* (the notion of food and medicine having the same origin). This television show has recorded an astonishing viewing rate of 57 percent, and popular interest in royal cuisine as well as traditional food has skyrocketed. Rows of titles on *gungjung eumsik,* or court cuisine, can now be found on the shelves of bookshops, and there have been official efforts to reconstruct and preserve royal cuisine as an Important National Intangible Cultural Property (No. 38), with the associated skills inherited by state-designated individuals (mainly former court maids) (Moon 2010; Bok-ryeo Han 2004).

At the same time, South Korea enjoys a lively and diverse food scene. Even a quick glance at the food section of a bookstore will reveal a wide variety of publications: a volume introducing medicinal diets believed to help individuals to live with cancer (Ok-kyeong Kim 2009); another describing a series of journeys to Buddhist temple kitchens for the purpose of tasting simple and pious meals (Ham 2010); yet another depicting efforts to locate environmentally sustainable healthy foods (Seon-mi Kim 2010); a manual offering suggestions for using traditional cooking and medicinal knowledge to transform family dinners (Kim and Yi 2010); a fashionable collection of essays accompanied by creative yet simple recipes written by a beautiful young TV chef (Pak 2006); and so on. As has always been the case in postwar Korea, Seoul streets continue to be filled with mobile food stalls, typically operated by middle-aged female vendors serving passersby hot kebabs or rice rolls. At five o'clock on a weekday evening, it is normal in Seoul to see men and women on their way home from their offices standing eating kebabs in front of street stalls in their business suits, bent over so as to avoid dribbling sauce onto their clothes. It is also common to see rice-cake sellers roaming around inside subway cars, filling the air with the temptingly sweet aroma of red bean paste. Spread out immediately outside the old city walls, Seoul's markets begin to open around three or four o'clock in the morning. The largest of these is Dongdaemun (East Gate) Market, followed by Namdaemun (South Gate) Market. These and the many other markets throughout the city are filled with all kinds of goods, including a large variety of freshly made, prepackaged, dried, and preserved food items. While markets in Korea have been lively locations since premodern times, found both in urban and rural areas (Chung 2006), the sheer volume and variety of food items available at East Gate and South Gate Markets is amazing; one could easily conclude from a trip to one of these two markets that it would be possible to buy almost anything there, from rare spices to obscure parts of edible animals. Markets also contain a large number of small eateries, often squeezed into narrow spaces between blocks of small stores or in back alleys. If one such eatery were featured on an evening television program, a long line of customers would be sure to form outside it the following day.

Seoul is also literally brimming with ethnic restaurants offering cuisine from virtually every corner of the world (Bak 2010). However, the image presented in the last two paragraphs is a deceptive one, suggesting that South Koreans no longer eat because they are hungry but rather in order to exercise a lifestyle choice. In fact, just as in the United States, there is a widening gap between rich and poor, and abundance and affluence remain the preserve of the upper echelons of society. According to an OECD survey, Korea's relative poverty (the rate of the population living on less than half the national median income) hit the 15 percent mark in 2008 (OECD 2012).

Korean Food Comes to America

In terms of typology, and I hasten to clarify that the terms I use below are basically working definitions, so-called American food and so-called Korean food appear to exhibit notable differences. On the American table, food is shared, both main and side dishes, eaters filling their plates as the food is passed around, whereas a Korean meal is structured around the individual table setting, which includes a portion of each dish allocated to each person. Further, the main course in an American meal usually consists of a large chunk of meat accompanied by side dishes; a proper meal in Korea consists of rice and soup along with a number of prepared dishes, including meat and vegetable. The most important ingredient in American food is meat, whereas Korean food has an unspecified combination of meat and vegetables, making it hard to determine whether meat occupies a prime position in Korean food. It is also difficult simply to reduce rice to the status of a side dish, as no Korean meal is complete without it. So, what happens when Korean food reaches America?

Of course, when we eat Korean food in the United States we are not eating Korean food as it is currently produced and consumed in Korea at this time. As is the case for other ethnic foods, Korean food is Americanized—whatever this might mean—prepared and served in such a way as to make it more familiar and accessible to American consumers—whoever they might be—while preserving a sufficient level of exoticness to promote its unique attributes. While the roots of Korean food in America vary according to region, class, or occasion (such as in the case of ritual or seasonal feasts), it often loses its idiosyncrasies through this process of Americanization, shifting to fit the frame of what the American food market expects of it. This in itself does not mean that Korean food in the United States is homogeneous. On the contrary, one finds striking differences between Korean food items served in different restaurants in different parts of this country. For example, the extent of the Korean presence in a particular region leads to significant differences in the way in which Korean food is marketed there. Alternatively, the targeted clientele available in a particular district may define and determine the taste of the Korean food offered there. Thus, while the regional origins of a particular dish may be confounded with and submerged under the loosely defined category of "Korean food," it may retain some of its unique characteristics, depending on the locality in which it is served, while continuing to adapt to regional and local markets (as will be shown in subsequent chapters). Furthermore, the routes by which a particular Korean food item has been brought to the United States will also have an influence on its later adaptation and transformation within the U.S. market. For example, the Korean cooking that was introduced to the United States by military brides would have gone through a process of adaptation and improvisation in order to suit the needs of particular families (Yuh 2002).

Following a diverse range of trajectories, Korean food is becoming part of American food. For example, a recent PBS series on Korean food called "Kimchi Chronicles" portrayed a productive and exciting meeting of Korean and American foods and cultures—whatever those terms may mean. Hosted by the attractive and inspiring Marja Vongerichten, who was born to a Korean mother and an African American father and adopted into an American family as a child, and her super-chef husband, Jean-George Vongerichten, the series literally broadcast a taste of Korea to the world (see http://www.kimchichronicles.tv/; Vongerichten 2011).

In this book, I write about four locations in the United States: Los Angeles, Baltimore, Hawai'i (divided into Kona on the island of Hawai'i and Honolulu on Oahu), and Iowa City. The food that I deal with here comes primarily from restaurants and grocery stores. In other words, home-cooked meals are excluded from my study. I visited restaurants and grocery stores in the above locations, making ethnographic observations. But, above all, I ate. My samples are by no means exhaustive or comprehensive, my strategy being rather to highlight a "theme" food item in each location, looking at its history, movement, and metamorphosis in the context of today's globalizing world. These theme food items include *naengmyeon* or chilled noodle soup in Los Angeles; *jeon* or pan-fried cakes (with vegetables, meat, or seafood) in Baltimore; *galbi* or barbecued beef, in Hawai'i; and *bibimbap,* a bowl in which rice is served with vegetables and some meat, in Iowa City. During my fieldwork, I myself acted as the primary "taster." As such, accounts relating to flavor, seasoning, texture, and other aspects of the experience of eating particular items largely derive from my own impressions. I also draw upon the insights of a few fellow-eaters in each location and one research assistant who sampled Korean food in Los Angeles, and their commentaries also form part of my interpretation of the foods presented here. At the same time, each chapter is a journey of its own, weaving its way through a unique fabric of diverse topics, including diaspora, immigration, colonialism, race, gender, diversity, globalization, and capitalism.

The reader must be wondering about the reasons for my selection of these particular food items and locations. My choices evolved from ongoing meetings between my own gastronomic trajectory and my immigrant experience as a member of the global Korean diaspora. In this sense, the subtitle of this book—"Gastronomic Ethnography of Authenticity"—carries a weighty meaning; for this book relies on what George Marcus named multisited ethnography as it follows the path taken by Korean food and the transformations it undergoes along the way (Marcus 1995), at the same time following my stomach (to put it bluntly) rather than anyone else's, in addition to my life trajectories. Los Angeles was chosen because it was the very first Koreatown in the United States that I happened to visit while working as a postdoctoral fellow at the Australian National University. Baltimore is the first American city I lived and worked in, spending nine years based there; I became mother of two in Baltimore, which inevitably influenced my eating experience. Iowa City was my home at the time of conducting research for this book, and therefore I was placed in an advantageous position to observe a newly emerged phenomenon involving rapidly increasing international students from Asia and their food consumption. I chose Kona in Hawai'i, on the other hand, in order to see how the U.S. annexation of Hawai'i in 1898 and Japan's annexation of Korea in 1910 led to an uneven appreciation of Korean food in Hawai'i and Japan; and I studied Korean food in Honolulu, with its waves of Japanese tourists, in order to understand how Korean food reinvents itself through its encounters with tourists, and to provide a basis for comparison with the invisibility of Korean food in Kona. These selections also reflect my dual origin: growing up in Japan as the child of Korean colonial immigrants and now living in the United States as a Korean American. As I began my fieldwork, or more precisely, as I began eating Korean foods at various places, I realized that I was using my primordial experience of having eaten Korean food in Japan as a reference point. At each of these locations, I tried to talk to the food I encountered—if I may use such an odd choice of terms—asking it where it came from and how it had ended up in this place and in this form, being consumed by someone like me.

At the same time, this book concerns the notion of authenticity—the regional, ethnic, and above all, national—authenticity of food. By visiting each of the above locations and eating Korean food at each, I built up an interesting set of questions regarding this concept, but I will postpone my full discussion of authenticity until the Conclusion, though nevertheless posing relevant questions along the way. Questions such as: When a food item travels across the globe, can it retain its authenticity? Or does authenticity in fact mean something other than simply being original? What is authenticity after all?

I must clarify that this book is not about Koreans or Korean communities in the United States. Though there would be no cuisine without people and communities, this book nevertheless focuses on the food itself—its trajectories, its journeys, and its stories, produced and inscribed as they are in national histories and in the global network of human flow and the relations of power. Therefore, I do not explore the inner worlds of the individual Koreans, Americans, or other eaters of Korean food introduced in this book. Similarly, though in itself it is a fascinating topic, it is also beyond the scope of this book to investigate exactly how individual Korean food items came to reach certain parts of the United States. Rather, my strategy here is to give my readers a sense of the way in which Korean food is consumed at my fieldwork sites and enable them to see that the Korean food we are looking at may not be quite so Korean after all. Indeed, the image I wish to convey in this book is one of Korean food metamorphosing in the context of national history and globalization. This image is not a still one: each of the food items that we encounter in this book has already undergone multiple iterations and incarnations, and is continuing its evolution into something else while retaining its identity (as contradictory as this may sound) as an example of Korean food. For example, this transformation is at times driven by a sheer lack of the proper ingredients in a foreign land or at times by market demand. Furthermore, this image in itself counters both nationalist arguments that each nation has its own authentic food, on one hand, and the notion of freedom of choice so prevalent on the U.S. food scene, on the other.

Mary Douglas once wrote:

If language is a code, where is the precoded message? The question is phrased to expect the answer: nowhere. . . . But try it this way: if food is a code, where is the precoded message? . . . If food is treated as a code, the messages it encodes will be found in the pattern of social relations being expressed. The message is about different degrees of hierarchy, inclusion and exclusion, boundaries and transactions across the boundaries. (Douglas 1972: 61)

In writing about the examples of Korean food that I found at selected locations throughout the United States, I will try to do something similar to what Douglas had in mind: decipher the message or story told by the food and see what kinds of social relations and historical conditions it speaks to and of. This is a message generated by the sociohistorical field, itself in turn defined by and laden with uneven power relations between nations, classes, and individuals. This is also a message involving boundaries and their transgression—boundaries between nation-states, between classes, genders, and so on. As such, we may find that there is no such thing as "authentic" food—Korean or otherwise—that neatly fits within the national boundaries that remain to this day.

1 | A Global Slurp

Naengmyeon Noodles

Koreatown, Los Angeles

It is easy to forget that you are in America as you walk through Los Angeles' Koreatown surrounded by Korean language signs of different types and sizes. Greater Los Angeles has the largest Korean American population in the country (over 334,000 in 2010). To put this figure in context, there were 1,042,580 Korean-born immigrants in the country as a whole in 2007 (Terrazas 2009). This district featured widely on the world news scene in 1992 when it became the center of mass rioting and looting in the violent aftermath of the acquittal of police officers involved in the brutal attack on the African American Rodney King. The violence spread throughout South Central Los Angeles, eventually leading to the targeting of stores and properties owned by Koreans and other Asians. A total of fifty-three persons were killed, more than two thousand injured, and thousands of fires recorded, with Korean American businesses suffering a total damage bill of approximately $350 million (Abelmann and Lie 1997: 8). Koreatown became a primary target of the riots: countless Korean stores were looted, destroyed, and set on fire, while an unknown number of Korean individuals were attacked, brutalized, and subjected to racial violence. On the second day of the riots, rioters succeeded in overpowering National Guards, police, and firefighters, who abandoned Koreatown and left storekeepers there in a position where they had to defend themselves. By the sixth day, order had begun to be restored, but not before irreparable damage and destruction had taken place.

In the aftermath of the LA riots, Koreatown had to make tremendous efforts in order to rebuild and reunite. Not only did the community face the task of physical reconstruction, but also, perhaps even more important, that of remaking its image as a lively shopping district. Korean business owners made a concerted effort to revitalize the district in solidarity with other ethnic and racial groups. Indeed, Koreatown in Los Angeles is one of the most racially diverse districts in the United States, with 23 percent of the population claiming Korean ancestry and 22 percent Mexican ancestry. Los Angeles is the most populous city in the state of California. According to Edward Chang, more than a quarter-million Korean Americans live in the metropolitan region that includes Los Angeles, Orange County, and San Bernardino-Ventura (Chang 2003). The 2010 U.S. Census found that 11.3 percent of a total of 3,792,621 persons in the city of Los Angeles had Asian origins and 48.5 percent Hispanic or Latino origins. Koreans are not the most numerous Asian ethnic group in southern California; Chinese Americans outnumber them by 150,000 (Nadia Kim 2008: 117). As far as Koreatown is concerned, however, one immediately notes the overwhelmingly Korean visual presence. Hundreds of stores—restaurants, groceries, nighttime establishments, supermarkets, bookstores, souvenir stores, traditional costume tailors, beauty salons, bridal shops, insurance agencies, physicians' offices, Korean-owned hotels, and many other businesses coexist in this district, appealing to both Korean and non-Korean customers from within Los Angeles and beyond, from other parts of the United States and overseas.

I visited LA's Koreatown for the first time in 1995, three years after the riots. There were many new buildings, and many of the older ones had been extensively refurbished in the wake of the destruction suffered. On a site located at pretty much the middle of Koreatown stood a new Korea Plaza. I went in and discovered a small, friendly eatery serving items from a familiar Korean menu filled with typical staple items—*ojingeo bokkeum* (sautéed spicy calamari), *bibimbap* (a bowl of rice mixed with vegetables and sometimes with meat), *bulgogi* (barbecued beef), and so on. Having just flown fourteen hours from Sydney—I was a research fellow at the Australian National University at the time—I was struggling a little with jet lag, but was pleasantly surprised at the unexpectedly warm climate in December—it was the first time I had visited the U.S. West Coast and had not been fully aware of its stable temperate climate. As this small restaurant looked friendly, even quite inviting, I did not hesitate to go in.

As soon as I was seated, small plates of appetizers and side dishes began arriving one after another, a practice familiar to U.S. connoisseurs of

Korean food. I had not been initiated into this method of serving, but I now also realize, in retrospect, that they were giving me a larger number of dishes than usual, either because they were trying to compete against other similar establishments in the area, or (as I prefer to think) because they wanted to be kind to this visitor who was looking quite lost and spoke English with a British accent and Korean with a Japanese one. I was overwhelmed: my table was already filled with little plates containing napa cabbage *kimchi,* cucumber *kimchi,* seaweed vinaigrette salad, radish salad, sweet anchovies, potato salad, steamed vegetables mixed with hot *yangnyeom* (pesto-like thick and spicy sauce), sweet and spicy dried calamari salad, and so on. Wondering whether I had been misunderstood when placing my order in a language jumbled with foreign accents, I began to eat. Before I knew it, I found myself devouring all of the dishes. After a short while, a pleasant young woman came up to my table with rice, soup, and the main dish of *ojingeo bokkeum.* Noticing that I'd cleaned up most of the little plates, she went off and returned with more plates of *kimchi,* placing them in front of me with a friendly smile. Behind the counter, I noticed a man who looked like her father doing the cooking and a woman who looked like her mother working nearby. It was a typical mom-and-pop operation, and I imagined the woman to be their daughter, perhaps helping them out part-time while attending college. The food was simply delicious.

When I returned to the same plaza sixteen years later in 2011, I hoped to find the same restaurant again. I imagined that by now the young woman would have left town to attend a graduate program or a professional school somewhere else but that her parents would surely be still there; I even remembered the tangy, spicy taste of their *ojingeo bokkeum* and felt my mouth begin to water. It came as a big disappointment, therefore, when I entered the plaza and was unable to find a trace of their little eatery. Facing me instead was a standard American mall-style food court. The plaza had obviously been upgraded. It was much more modern, if you like, matching the mall culture of the contemporary United States. The lower ground floor contained a large supermarket, while the upper level was occupied by specialty stores, including a bookstore, a jeweler, a pottery and craft store, a coffee shop, and so on. The food court occupied the ground floor. Although store fronts were presented in an American style, the food being served was unmistakably Korean, albeit with additional Asian items such as Vietnamese noodle soup, a dish that is actually very popular in Korea today. As I looked around, I was glad to see a stand serving *naengmyeon,* my favorite Korean chilled noodle soup *(naeng* denoting cold or chilled and *myeon* meaning noodles). Just like similar stands at any food court in Korea, this stand specialized exclusively in *naengmyeon.* Even the price was similar to that in Korea: the dish would cost around $7 or $8 at a food court in Seoul, here in Los Angeles I paid $5.50.

According to the practice of a food court, I placed my order and paid for my meal, taking a seat at one of the tables clustered around the middle of the space. It was a little after lunch hour. I could see that the other customers were predominantly Korean: multigenerational families enjoying a lunch out together, a small group of business people chatting away after finishing their meal, a group of nicely dressed women laughing, and so on. When called, I stood up and went over to collect my order of *naengmyeon.* In common with the standard way of presenting *naengmyeon,* the tray contained a large bowl of noodles, a small bowl of *kimchi,* chopsticks, and a spoon. When I started to eat, however, a strange memory came back to me—not of the *naengmyeon* I had eaten a few months earlier at a food court in Seoul, which I thought would have been the most natural association, but of the *naengmyeon* I had had in Pyongyang decades earlier. Just like in Pyongyang, and unlike in Seoul, this bowl of *naengmyeon* was made with unbleached dark buckwheat noodles (see color plates).

From LA to Pyongyang

It was 1985. Summer that year in Pyongyang was hot but dry, making it altogether bearable. The boulevards were mostly empty and the air clean, perhaps due to the absence of a large volume of car exhaust fumes. We arrived, a busload of us, at Okryugwan (Crystal Stream House), the famous Pyongyang restaurant that had begun operating in 1960 (Lankov 2007: 90). Although exhibiting traditional design features, the restaurant had been built using modern materials—mostly concrete. Its distinct Asian-style green-tiled roof blended in beautifully in front of the rows of willow trees lining the banks of the Daedong River. Upon our arrival, we were seated in a huge banquet room as guests of state. This was one of numerous feasts that were offered to us during this visit to North Korea. I dined twice at Okryugwan, sampling its *jaengbanguksu* (tray noodles) and *mulnaengmyeon* (chilled noodle soup, *mul* literally meaning water). Both dishes use *memil* (buckwheat) noodles, which are extremely chewy (Cecilia Hae-Jin Lee 2009: 135).

These noodles are chewy because the buckwheat is mixed with starches, mostly from potatoes and sweet potatoes, but also from arrowroot. The *jaengbanguksu* was served on a huge, tray-sized plate. While basically containing the same ingredients as *mulnaengmyeon,* it had only a minimal soup component and was more like a dish served au jus. Both contained one or two thin slices of beef, a small amount of cabbage *kimchi* with a minimal amount of red pepper, and a slice or two of Asian pear. While both tasted more or less the same, the fact that one had been soaked in soup and the other presented on a tray made eating each of them a different experience. While I gave no consideration to this issue at the time, I can now appreciate how much electricity was required in order to prepare and serve chilled noodle dishes such as these to overseas visitors in the middle of summer. This is because *naengmyeon* tastes best after being refrigerated for several hours (Hepinstall 2001: 87). It is also one of the reasons why *naengmyeon* is a food-court favorite in Seoul: stores can have it ready and serve it quickly, almost at the pace of a McDonald's drive-thru. Almost all of the food courts that I visited in Seoul had *naengmyeon* stands, in almost all cases prepared using white, bleached noodles.

The noodles I had in Los Angeles, however, were dark, just like those I had tried all those years ago in Pyongyang. I assumed that this was based on the belief that dark noodles, like whole wheat bread, were healthier, having undergone a lesser amount of processing. But the reason this dish reminded me of Pyongyang *naengmyeon* was more closely related to its broth, or *yuksu*—notably, the distinct lack of the artificial MSG (monosodium glutamate)-like flavor that one would normally taste in prepackaged or so-called instant *naengmyeon* broth you can buy at Korean grocery stores. The flavor of MSG is hard to describe. Its original Japanese inventors in the early twentieth century called it *umami,* distinguishing it from the four basic tastes: sweet, salty, sour, and bitter. The *umami* flavor was extracted from a kind of seaweed, *konbu* or Laminaria japonica, the taste of which I am very familiar with, having grown up in Japan (Kurihara 2009). MSG-oriented flavor enhancers or broth additives have been widely used in Japan since the early twentieth century and were introduced to Korea during the colonial period (1910–1945). Today, one can find many variants on the shelves of supermarkets in Korea, as well as in Koreatowns throughout the United States (Yamaguchi and Ninomiya 1998; Lindemann, Ogiwara, and Ninomiya 2002).

At this *naengmyeon* stall in Koreatown in Los Angeles, however, I could not detect any trace of this taste that was so familiar to me. It was only upon exiting the food court that I noticed the large sign "No MSG." It made sense. This Japanese invention, which reached Korea during the period of Japanese colonial rule, was not available in North Korea in 1985, while in Los Angeles in 2011 there was a self-imposed avoidance of MSG, presumably for health reasons. Recent studies have shown mixed results regarding the effects of MSG on health. While some reports link consumption of MSG to obesity, others claim that there is no relationship between MSG and weight gain (Bakalar 2008; Freeman 2006; Shi et al. 2010). This issue aside, it was ironic to see and taste *naengmyeon* similar to that which I had had in Pyongyang way back in 1985 at a Koreatown food court in Los Angeles in 2011. It is not my intention, however, to attribute the similarity between the *naengmyeon* dishes I enjoyed in Los Angeles and Pyongyang solely to their lack of MSG. It is conceivable, for example, that the *naengmyeon* stand owner in the Koreatown food court originally came from northern Korea. While no conclusive connection can be drawn, it is nevertheless true that tasting Pyongyang *naengmyeon* in Koreatown, LA, thousands of miles away and many decades later, was as much a transcendental as a global experience.

A Northern Delicacy

Naengmyeon is a cold delicacy originating in the northern part of the Korean peninsula, a curious fact when one considers that this part of the peninsula has a colder climate than the south. Furthermore, according to *Dongguk sesigi* or *The Seasonal Record of the Eastern Countries*, a book written during the nineteenth century on culinary and other everyday cultures of the Joseon, the last Korean dynasty (1392–1910), *naengmyeon* was a winter food, combining buckwheat and starch noodles, radish *kimchi*, cabbage *kimchi*, and pork slices in a bowl (Bok-ryeo Han 2004: 110). It explains how the premodern Korean *naengmyeon* could have been served chilled. In her reminiscences about her late grandfather, popular South Korean TV chef and culinary essayist Pak Jae-eun recalls how her grandfather, a refugee from the north who came to the south during the Korean War, enjoyed *naengmyeon* all year round throughout his entire life (Pak 2006: 116). Today, most Korean recipe books refer to *naengmyeon* as a summer food. One such publication claims that the dish gives one "a brief respite from the intense heat of the Korean summer" (Chun and Baek 2004: 53), while another notes that: "At lunch hour, office workers, businessmen, and shoppers pack the [*naengmyeon*] houses throughout Korea, slurping away in the summer heat" (Hepinstall 2001: 87).

Naengmyeon is typically divided into two varieties: *mulnaengmyeon,* or soup noodle, which has a chilled broth; and *bibimnaengmyeon,* which consists of cold noodles mixed with spicy vegetables and meat, and might be referred to as a kind of noodle salad (Kazuko and Song 2010: 305). Pyongyang is known for its *mulnaengmyeon,* while Hamheung, another northern city, is known for its *bibimnaengmyeon.* In many restaurants throughout South Korea, a waitress will bring a pair of scissors when presenting you with a bowl of *mulnaengmyeon,* offering to cut the noodles for you. If requested to do so, she then sticks the scissors into the bowl and cuts the noodles in a few places. This additional service is offered in order to make the dish easier to eat, as the noodles used in its preparation have an incredibly chewy texture. As stated above, *mulnaengmyeon* is typically served with *kimchi,* slices of Asian pear, and one or two very thin slices of meat (most likely lean beef or pork). According to the royal chronicles, when *naengmyeon* was prepared for the king, it was garnished with pine-nut kernels and pomegranates and mixed with powdered chili, pig's feet (or slices thereof), in addition to pears and *kimchi. Naengmyeon* became part of the regular *surasang* menu (see Introduction) for the king's table toward the end of the Joseon dynasty (1392–1910) (Bok-ryeo Han 2004: 110).

Being a northern delicacy, *naengmyeon* often uses a favorite northern form of *kimchi* called *dongchimi,* which can best be described as water *kimchi.* Radishes or cabbages (radishes being preferred) are coarsely sliced into lumps and salted, then mixed into a broth with a base of chilled fish, shellfish, or seaweed along with *saeujeot* (tiny salted shrimp). The mixture is then stored in a cool place, but for a considerably shorter time than would be the case with regular *kimchi.* (Smothered in red chili powder, the latter is packed into earthen jars and often buried underground to be consumed over the winter.) Water *kimchi* is not as garlicky as regular red *kimchi* either. Rather, it is more pungent than hot and spicy. While in itself a great side dish, when used as a topping for *naengmyeon,* its juice mixes with the noodle broth, emitting a pungent and tangy taste due to its fermentation. Han Bok-ryeo, the leading Korean specialist on royal cuisine, recommends that *dongchimi* radishes should be sliced very thin and mixed with salted, sliced cucumber before being sautéed in a lightly greased pan and allowed to cool before being placed on top of the noodles. She refers to this dish as *dongchi-miguksu* (*dongchimi* noodles), rather than simply *naengmyeon*. According to Han's recipe, the preparation of *naengmyeon* involves two different kinds of broth: meat broth and *kimchi* juice (itself based on a fish- or shellfish-based broth). The Asian pear, Han remarks, was the favorite ingredient of King Gojong, the penultimate king of the Joseon dynasty, who enjoyed *naeng-myeon* as a nighttime meal. Whether it was the king's favorite or not, *mul-naengmyeon* only became popular in southern Korea after the Korean War (1950–1953), a development I suspect was related to the relocation of millions of northerners to the south as refugees during these years. In order to avoid U.S. air raids, millions of people fled to the south with minimal amounts of their personal belongings. Although they could not bring much else with them, often becoming separated from or losing family members during their journey, they did bring *naengmyeon* to the south. Seen in this way, this dish's arrival in the south as a popular food item bears a close association with the bloody history of the peninsula.

Global *Naengmyeon*

Earlier, I touched on my dining experiences at Okryugwan (Crystal Stream House), a Pyongyang restaurant famed for its *naengmyeon*. More recently, reflecting the economic impasse that North Korea has faced for some time, the North Korean government has begun opening and operating overseas branches of this restaurant, particularly in China. According to a Japanese news outlet, there are currently nine North Korean–operated restaurants in Beijing, twelve in Shenyang, four in Dalian, and eight in Dandong, a city located right across the Yalu River from North Korea. These restaurants have been gaining popularity among ethnic Koreans living in China as well as South Korean businessmen and foreign diplomats. The South Korean government is wary of its nationals frequenting North Korean establishments overseas. Suspecting that these restaurants may be functioning as bases for intelligence gathering by the North Korean government, the South Korean government has requested that its nationals in China restrain themselves from visiting North Korean restaurants ("Kitachōsen resutoran" 2010).

According to Oh Tae-jin of the South Korean newspaper *Chosun Ilbo*, the first branch of Okryugwan to open in Beijing began operating in 2003; currently it makes a daily profit of more than seven million won (approximately $6,200) (Oh 2010). Oh also mentions the Okryugwan restaurant in Siem Reap, Cambodia, as a media hot spot, because "a beautiful waitress [there] gained near-celebrity status in South Korea" after her picture was posted and circulated on the Internet (Oh 2010). At another Okryugwan in Deira, Dubai, all of the waitresses wear "North Korean flags on their blouses" (Croucher and Huang 2010). According to Martin Croucher and Carol Huang, the Okryugwan chain now has branches in Nepal and Thailand as well. Indeed, one commentator wrote: "North Korea's best-known exports tend to be conventional weapons and nuclear technology. But now, curious diners can add . . . noodles to that list, thanks to a chain of North Korean restaurants in China, Nepal, Thailand and Dubai" (Kenyon 2010).

The year 1999 saw the opening of the restaurant's Seoul branch—or so it appeared from first announcements. Many people lined up patiently awaiting their turn to take a seat at this relatively small restaurant. Since opening in May of that year, the Seoul Okryugwan had to turn away as many as three thousand customers a day due to a lack of seating ("Great Leader" 1999). Contrary to the initial public understanding that the restaurant was a North Korean-franchised operation, it later became clear that it was owned by a Korean entrepreneur in Japan with connections to the pro–North Korea expatriate organization there and staffed by a chef who had defected from the north (Kirk 1999). North Korea swiftly issued an official denial of any connection with the Seoul Okryugwan (In-ku Kim 1999; "Seoul Branch" 1999). In the meantime, North Korea also tried to come up with its own new version of *naengmyeon,* opening the Songsan Sikdang (Songsan restaurant) in the early 2000s at Mangyeongdae, the official birthplace of deceased President Kim Il Sung, who had been posthumously appointed as Eternal President (Ryang 2012). According to a North Korean news outlet, several thousand customers had visited this restaurant because it offered original noodles prepared *jachejeogeuro* (following its own initiative—a North Korean cliché), using its own unique broth, soup, and spices ("Pyongyang Okryugwan" 2005). Whether the Songsan *naengmyeon* at Mangyeongdae offers a more revolutionary flavor (so to speak) than that offered by Okryugwan in Pyongyang is hard to determine. However, the opening of the former restaurant is clearly part of efforts to elevate and maintain the image of Kim Il Sung's birthplace as an all-benefiting legendary site, a common practice in North Korea.

On the other hand, it is not in Pyongyang or at Mangyeongdae that one can supposedly enjoy the best *bibimnaengmyeon* (a spicy *naengmyeon* salad mixed with vegetables and meat), but in Hamheung. This city in southern Hamgyeong Province is one of North Korea's major industrial sites, and is known for its textile production. *Bibimnaengmyeon* has no soup, but is mixed with a pesto-like substance containing a hot and spicy sauce made from ingredients such as chili powder, garlic, and bean paste. To this mixture are added various vegetables, such as squash, cucumbers, mushrooms, radishes, and so on, along with the meat of one's choice—all of the ingredients being thinly sliced. This dish is similar to *bibimbap*, a rice dish served in a bowl with sliced vegetables and meat that are also mixed with spices and hot sauce (see Chapter 4). Here, the use of oil becomes important. Whereas *mulnaengmyeon* hardly uses any oil, except in the recipe by Han noted above in which *dongchimi* and cucumber slices are lightly sautéed—a rare recommendation—*bibimnaengmyeon* uses sesame seed oil. The addition of this oil not only enhances the flavor and aroma of the dish, but also makes it easier to mix the noodles.

On my journey to North Korea in 1985, our group was not allowed to visit Hamheung, but I was able to make a visit to a coal miner's family in nearby Gowon. The County Party organization had arranged meals and accommodation for me prior to my arrival. On arriving in the town (along with my "supervisor"—all foreign visitors have to be accompanied by someone in North Korea, usually a party official), I was first invited to an official welcoming feast. Laid out on a table in humble fashion were many potato-based dishes: boiled and sautéed potatoes, some salty, some spicy, but hardly any sweet ones, sugar being a precious commodity in North Korea. In addition, there were hardly any dishes with complicated blends of herbs and spices, these ingredients also being hard to find. A little way into the feast, following a welcome address by a local party representative, young women brought in shallow bowls of *bibimnaengmyeon* for everyone. At the sight of the *bibimnaengmyeon,* even local party officials looked excited. I could tell that this was a rare treat for them. Many gasped in surprise when they saw that the dish was garnished with egg mimosa. No one came up with scissors to help me separate my noodles, but I relished their rubbery chewiness along with the sight of the happy expressions on the faces of the locals. Mixed with a minimal amount of chopped vegetables in a mildly spicy sauce, the noodles had hardly any flavor, potato starch giving them a rubbery consistency, yet the meal was delicious and certainly filled me up. Interestingly, no one called it *bibimnaengmyeon* or *naengmyeon*. Instead, the local North Koreans referred to it as *gamjaguksu*, or potato noodles.

Noodle Varieties

Koreans did not enjoy noodles until relatively recent times. Historically, Korea did not have a tradition of wheat cultivation, and grain was imported from China during the Goryeo dynasty (the tenth to thirteenth centuries), making wheat noodles an expensive commodity (Choi et al. 2007: 25). While buckwheat was relatively easy to grow, potatoes only began to be imported from China during the early nineteenth century, making it likely that a more traditional starch such as arrowroot may have been used in the production of *naengmyeon* noodles (Jo 2001: 16). As noted above, this dish remained a northern delicacy and did not achieve nationwide diffusion until the middle of the twentieth century. This pattern is quite different from that found in Japan or China, where wheat noodles became a staple food from a much earlier period. In Japan, for example, *udon* noodles made from wheat flour and *soba* noodles made from buckwheat flour have been popular staples for centuries (e.g., Watanabe 1992). Today, noodles are found everywhere in the Korean diet, saturating market places, eateries, and homes. In Seoul, small noodle houses fill the corners of markets, and stands selling noodle-based dishes occupy most of the prominent spots in food courts. *Ramyeon,* or instant noodles, are frequently consumed in a wide variety of locations, from private homes to PC cafes and college dormitories. Meanwhile, in the United States, it is Japanese *rāmen* that dominate supermarket shelves. Anyone who has visited an Asian food store in the United States will have noticed dozens of packets of instant noodles from Japan, China, and Korea. Even in the "Asian/International Food" aisles of regular supermarkets, one can find packets of soup noodles—predominantly Japanese, but with an increasing number of Korean, Chinese, and Vietnamese (*pho*) varieties. As such, it appears that *rāmen* noodle soup has attained the status of a global food.

Momofuku Ando created the current easy-to-eat version of instant *rāmen* noodle soup in Japan in 1958 (Fabrizio, Potineni, and Gray 2010: 141). A half-century later, Asian noodles have become one of the most popular ethnic cuisine trends in the United States ("Noodles in the US" 2013). In the meantime, many interesting innovations have been applied to the production of instant noodles, including ingredients, seasoning, noodle texture, convenience, and branding. Generally speaking, seasoning components include a high proportion of salt, in addition to MSG, sugar, soy sauce, corn syrup, garlic, onions, oils, starches, yeasts, hydrolyzed vegetable or animal proteins, acids, anti-caking agents, and artificial and natural flavors (Fabrizio, Potineni, and Gray 2010: 142). The science and technology of instant noodle soup production is all about ensuring convenience, speed, and above all, an inexpensive purchase price.

In his fascinating article on *ramyeon* or Korean instant noodles, prominent Korean anthropologist Han Kyung-Koo makes some interesting points about noodle culture in Korea (Han 2010). Han claims that Korean *ramyeon*, with its spicy and distinctly chili-based flavor, has gained the status of a global food quite separate from Japanese *rāmen*. He asserts that this may be related to historical differences in the way Chinese food was disseminated in Japan and Korea. In Japan, Chinese food spread from around the time of the Sino-Japanese War (1894–1895), with restaurants specializing in Chinese cuisine found in a wide range of locations in addition to Chinatown districts. By contrast, though Chinese food certainly existed in Korea during colonial times, it was confined exclusively to small Chinatown areas. In general, even to this day, Chinese restaurants in Korea have been looked down upon, their standards of cleanliness viewed as suspect (Young-Kyun Yang 2010). Thus, in some ways, Korean *ramyeon* did not develop as a substitute for a Chinese food (as was the case with Japanese *rāmen*), instead developing as a uniquely Korean food from the outset.

For many years, the Samyang Corporation enjoyed a monopoly in the *ramyeon* market, holding a 40 percent share during the 1980s. Since facing a scandal in 1989, when it was discovered as using industrial tallow in the production of its *ramyeon,* the company has lost its lead ranking, and Nongshim Ramyeon Co. today enjoys domination of the instant *ramyeon* market. The latter company now exports 161 billion won–worth of instant *ramyeon* to more than seventy countries worldwide, enjoying a market share exceeding 60 percent in Korea (Kyung-Koo Han 2010: 64, 71). At any rate, popularity of *ramyeon* noodles in Korea is unmistakable, given its ubiquitous presence in supermarkets, convenience stores, college dorms, clubhouses, offices, and restaurants in Seoul. Han captures the Korean love of *ramyeon* in insightful ways:

During their years of schooling and military service, many Koreans eat a huge amount of *ramyeon* [as snacks, for example] and develop strange ways of serving it. As so many people developed an addiction to *ramyeon* as children, students, and soldiers, *ramyeon* plays a role in modifying class distinctions, instead of delineating and reinforcing [them] as food usually does. This class bonding role in *ramyeon* consumption is very interesting. . . . Koreans from all different socioeconomic backgrounds have eaten the same instant *ramyeon*, which leaves little room for assigning class distinctions. (Kyung-Koo Han 2010: 75–76)

From this insight, Han draws the conclusion that *ramyeon* is "a class confuser" (Kyung-Koo Han 2010: 60). While this is certainly a very innovative way of interpreting food, I have reservations regarding this approach. Does the fact that persons with different class backgrounds all relish *ramyeon*, in itself, make *ramyeon* a factor leading to the confusion of class-based differentiation? Han's own article seems to suggest that the opposite may be true. He quotes the example of the young president of a conglomerate who, having just succeeded to his father's position, turns up his nose at *ramyeon,* dismissing it as poor people's food. His father, indignant at his son's attitude, slurps away at bowls of *ramyeon* in public. Here, *ramyeon* is used, not as a class confuser, but as quite a clear indicator of class differentiation. Unequivocally, *ramyeon* is poor men's food. The father's admonition to his son rests on this point: that he should not forget how poor people live. Even though he may regularly eat caviar, foie gras, Kobe steak, and tuna *nigiri,* for example, occasionally eating *ramyeon* will lead the son to remember his ordinary, working-class clients and his own family's humble beginnings. *Ramyeon* eaten as a reminder of someone else's poverty or of one's own distant impoverished past is surely very different from *ramyeon* eaten as an everyday meal, as the only thing one can afford to eat, or as something that one eats as a treat after a few days of not being able to buy any food at all.

Spicy Calamari, After All

On one of my many trips to Los Angeles during 2010 and 2011, I was not able to stay in Koreatown itself, partly due to the fact that there are only a limited number of hotels there, but also because the room rates at the one I had stayed at before and wanted to stay at again, an extremely pleasant establishment with impeccably clean sheets and towels, exceeded my state allowance. My efforts to look for a hotel within my budget led me in a westerly direction, and I ended up staying at Santa Monica Beach. The affordable yet good-quality accommodation I found there, combined with the relatively reasonable rates for car rental at LAX, made the decision to base myself in Santa Monica an easy one. I commuted to Koreatown following Wilshire Boulevard eastward, passing Beverly Hills on the way. Parking in Koreatown, however, turned out to be rather a challenge, leading me to attempt the journey on one particular day using public transportation. The thought of not having to spend half an hour looking for a parking space and then refeeding the meter every hour after that was a source of relief.

Taking a seat on the express bus for the forty-five-minute journey to Koreatown, I did not yet realize what I was getting into that day. A few stops after Rodeo Drive, an African American man boarded the bus. He appeared to be suffering from alcohol dependency and was wearing a pair of pants that were hanging down in a strangely loose manner—I wondered if he was missing his belt. He began swearing violently at a nearby young African American woman dressed in business clothes, showering her with all kinds of racial slurs. His voice grew louder and louder as I looked on, first in discomfort, and then in disgust. I continued watching, as did the other passengers on the bus, not knowing what to do.

The young African American woman kept her composure, not even looking at the man. When the bus reached my stop near Koreatown, I stood up to use the exit. At that point, the man stood up too, his movement causing his pants to completely fall down around his feet, exposing his genitals. It was only then that other passengers began to complain about him. As he was in front of me, I was worried that I might not be able to get off the bus, as other passengers, who included more white persons than persons of color, were starting to press the female driver—a Latina, I thought—to call the police. Some even volunteered to do so themselves. I was shocked: verbal violence directed against an African American woman by an African American man was acceptable but his exposing his genitals was not. I did not wait to see whether the police ended up coming or not. As I fought my way through the crowd in order to get off the bus and started walking southward toward Koreatown, I still felt a sense of bewilderment. For this incident had brought home to me the delicate and nuanced pattern of accord and discord between races and also within each racial group.

Perhaps because of the above incident, I paid special attention on that day to the boundaries that existed within Koreatown. The following scene demonstrates how such boundaries are created, reinforced, and contested. A shiny Mercedes Benz was parked alongside a Korean supermarket. An opulently dressed middle-aged woman came out of the store and unlocked the door of the car, revealing an incredibly well-groomed white puppy sporting a pink bow inside. The lady was wearing an Astrakhan bolero (despite the pleasant weather) and carrying a French designer purse, popular among Korean women in both Korea and Los Angeles. She hugged the puppy and happily drove off. At the exact spot she had just pulled away from, a homeless woman was squatting, picking up coins that people had accidentally dropped when feeding the parking meter. When the woman stood up, I noticed that she was Asian-looking too, quite possibly Korean. Wrapped in what seemed to be a dark-green blanket, again in spite of the very pleasant weather, her hair was greasy and her face looked as if it had not been washed in days or weeks. I was captured by the ironic correspondence between the rich woman's Astrakhan, worn as a fashion statement, and this woman's blanket, kept beside her for necessity—both worn in spite of the warm weather. I could not resist following the latter with my eyes. After passing a few vehicles, she picked up a paper coffee cup that appeared to contain some leftover beverage, and slowly moved toward a nearby intersection. Koreatown, a locale marked so thickly by ethnic culture, is also a place insurmountably divided along class boundaries.

Having already sampled a few restaurants and small eateries on previous visits to Koreatown, I decided to try a *sikdang*-style restaurant that day. This term, meaning "eating hall" and a direct translation of the Japanese term *shokudō*, most likely inserted itself into the Korean vocabulary during the period of Japanese colonial rule (1910–1945). A *sikdang* is a restaurant where one can eat home-style cooking, including generic Korean staples such as *bibimbap* (a bowl of rice mixed with vegetables and meat), *bulgogi* (barbecued beef), *pajeon* (leek pancakes), and, yes, *ojingeo bokkeum* (sautéed spicy calamari). As it was around 3:45 p.m., past lunchtime but too early for dinner, the restaurant was empty save for a curious anthropologist and a middle-aged man who I gathered must have been drinking for a while, as his happy face had turned red.

Two women appeared to be running the restaurant, one middle-aged and the other slightly older. When I entered, both of them were watching a Korean soap opera on television. I sat down and ordered *ojingeo bokkeum*.

The older woman, obviously the chef, stood up and went to the kitchen at the back, while the other woman began bringing out small plates of appetizers and side dishes. They looked fabulous: pickled radish, cucumber *kimchi,* fried and seasoned bean shoots, cabbage *kimchi,* seasoned perilla leaves, and so on. While I waited for my main course, the gentleman customer asked for another beer. To my surprise, the middle-aged woman turned around and said: "Haven't you had enough to drink, sir?" (*Sul jom mani deusingeo ganneyo?*) I was surprised, because talking to a customer in this manner would be considered unsophisticated in Korea today. The man kept on smiling as she served him another beer without further comment.

Then, my *ojingeo bokkeum* arrived, accompanied by a bowl of rice and another containing chilled bean-sprout soup. I dived in, hoping the meal would be as delicious as the one I had had back in 1995. This time, however, the taste was very different. Though I would still characterize it as delicious, it was a different kind of delicious. It was not as spicy or as tangy as the one I had had in 1995. Rather, it was sweeter and redder. On the other hand, I was very taken by the chilled bean-sprout soup, which was simply delightful. I found the combination of the cool broth, golden coloring, and nutty bean-sprout heads quite perfect, and it definitely reminded me of my mother's own version of this dish. (As my mother was born in Japan to Korean parents, I should really say that it was my grandmother's soup. I wondered if the older woman in the kitchen came from North Gyeongsang Province in southeastern Korea, just like my grandmother.) To my chagrin, having already sampled many different dishes that day, I was unable to finish the *ojingeo bokkeum.* But I happily finished the soup, using my spoon and not slurping from the bowl, the latter being a Japanese convention that older generations of Koreans in Japan frown upon. Not that anyone was watching—the two women had rushed back to their Korean soap opera immediately after serving my meal, while the happy gentleman continued to enjoy his beer.

The Strange Life of *Naengmyeon*

As already stated, I came across *naengmyeon* in Los Angeles purely by chance. In some ways, however, there is a reasonably convincing historical explanation for the way in which I encountered *naengmyeon* in Los Angeles in 2011. This dish reflects elements of Korean history such as national

partition, civil war, mass displacement, and then diaspora, having made its
way from the north of the Korean Peninsula to the south and then across
the Pacific to the United States. In a subtle yet unmistakable manner, the
unexpected similarities between versions of *naengmyeon* found in Pyongyang and Los Angeles can be traced back to the partition of the peninsula,
a situation worsened by a civil war that set one half of the Korean people
permanently against the other. As already discussed, noodles were a rare
item in medieval Korea, as wheat did not grow well there and had to be imported from China. During the late Joseon period in the nineteenth century, royalty was eating *naengmyeon*. As we saw, King Gojong enjoyed it
with lots of pears as a nighttime meal, one of the five meals that he enjoyed
each day. It was only after the Korean War of 1950–1953, which resulted in
millions of northerners fleeing to the south as refugees, that this northern
delicacy became part of southerners' everyday diet. In the meantime, food
shortages and economic difficulties back in North Korea meant that northerners were not able to eat their own native foods as frequently as before.
My 1985 visit to the North Korean mining town of Gowon revealed that
locals only rarely had the opportunity to enjoy chilled *gamjaguksu,* or potato noodles. As such, the *naengmyeon* in Los Angeles tells the story of national partition and displacement, diaspora and globalization, that Koreans
experienced during the latter half of the twentieth century.

In the strange journey taken by *naengmyeon,* we can identify multiple
layers of claims to authenticity by more than one entity. As South Korea's
favorite summer dish, *naengmyeon* clearly has a place on the South Korean
national menu today. Yet, even in South Korea, it is known that *naengmyeon* is a dish of northern origin. Thus, South Korean *naengmyeon*
products tend to bear the name Pyongyang (North Korea's capital) in
their brand names—as in *Pyongyangsik naengmyeon* or Pyongyang-style
naengmyeon—denoting its authenticity. When the purportedly North
Korean Okryugwan restaurant opened in Seoul, its popularity derived from
a desire among customers to taste authentic Pyongyang *naengmyeon*. Clearly,
Koreans themselves draw a distinction between more or less authentic
versions of *naengmyeon*. Yet, once it has crossed the national border, *naengmyeon* simply becomes Korean, regardless of whether it is considered
Pyongyang-style or not, as in the version found at the food court in Los Angeles's Koreatown. The irony here is that it did indeed resemble Pyongyang
naengmyeon, even after having half-circled the globe and been introduced into a health-conscious MSG-free U.S. ethnic food market. It is

also important to note here that the recent overseas expansion by North Korean *naengmyeon* restaurant businesses might well result in further contested claims of authenticity as this dish continues its penetration of the global food market.

The notion of authenticity takes a different turn if we turn to the example of *ramyeon* noodles. According to the article by Han Kyung Koo cited above, *ramyeon* is Korean and not a derivative of the Japanese dish *rāmen*. Indeed, there is a difference in the flavor of the soup: whereas Japanese *rāmen* is available in a variety of flavors, such as soy sauce or *miso* (bean curd), chicken or shrimp, Korean *ramyeon* tends to be simply hot and spicy. Its soup is also more or less always red due to the excessive use of dried red chili powder. However, can such differences be considered a sufficient basis for the claim that this dish has a discrete national identity? In fact, when Korean *ramyeon* packets reach U.S. supermarket shelves, they are thrown together with other, similar kinds of "instant noodles," including Chinese and Japanese ones, all displayed alongside each other in the International or Asian Food aisles. Here again, we witness national authenticity being infinitely compromised once a particular product has crossed its national border and entered the globalized food market.

If being authentic means being the same as the original, if not the original itself, how are we to understand the authenticity of the Pyongyang *naengmyeon* served at every food court in South Korea, or even of those versions found in LA's Koreatown and at other locations throughout the United States? Is it even conceivable to have authentic *naengmyeon* in South Korea since the partition of the peninsula and the severing of ties that had existed between northern and southern regions? One may claim that refugees paid for the transmission of *naengmyeon* to the south through the anguish they suffered at being forced to leave their ancestral homes and the pain and loss they endured as they left their northern home during the Korean War. Such an argument would, however, be immediately rejected by the current North Korean government, as its globalization strategy relies in part on the authenticity of Pyongyang-brand *naengmyeon*. It would seem, therefore, that the contest for national authenticity has reached an impasse when it comes to this particular dish: as long as Korea remains partitioned, *naengmyeon*, as it were, remains devoid of an authentic home.

2 | Food for the Ancestors

Jeon Pancakes

Koreans in Baltimore

Spread around an inlet near the top of Chesapeake Bay, Baltimore is a unique mid-Atlantic city. First settled by the Englishman David Jones in 1661, Baltimore has a long history of Colonial settlement. It played a key role in the events that led to the United States achieving independence from the United Kingdom and was also a center for the North American slave trade. The city continued to grow throughout the eighteenth and nineteenth centuries, not only in population and physical size, but also in economic, financial, and political importance. It was near the city's Fort McHenry that the British fleet was sunk during the War of 1814, inspiring Francis Scott Key to write a poem that later became the U.S. national anthem, *The Star-Spangled Banner*. Today, a monumental suspension bridge bearing Key's name links the northeastern and southeastern districts of the city across Chesapeake. According to census data, the city had a population of a little more than 620,000 persons in 2010, making it twentieth in size among U.S. cities. Extensively featured in David Harvey's book on postmodernism, Baltimore is known for its post-1960 urban renewal and its charming Inner Harbor, which includes the National Aquarium in addition to a number of typical franchise outlets such as Hard Rock Café (Harvey 1990). It is a racially and culturally diverse city, vibrant with ethnic enclaves and their various cuisines. Its restaurants also feature regional varieties of American dishes, probably the most famous being Maryland crab.

With its strong African American majority and the unique speech of its residents, Baltimore is often seen as part of the South. In 2010, only 2.3 percent of its population was classified as Asian. Nevertheless, when

I arrived in the city in 1997 to assume a position as an assistant professor of anthropology at The Johns Hopkins University, the shooting and killing of a Korean American college student by an African American four years earlier still came up regularly in conversation. Despite the testimonies of four witnesses identifying twenty-year-old African American Davon Neverdon as the person who had killed Joel Lee, a Korean American senior at Towson State University, and another witness who testified that Neverdon had bragged afterwards about the murder, the nearly all-black jury acquitted Neverdon in July 1995. After the acquittal Tucker Carlson wrote: "Korean-Americans aren't getting much sympathy from the Baltimore establishment. A *Baltimore Sun* editorial answered their [Korean Americans'] protests by blaming Koreans for black animosity. Unlike Italian and Jewish shopkeepers earlier in the century, the editorial intoned, Koreans 'have not been as successful in bridging the cultural and language gaps'" (Carlson 1995). In contrast to Carlson, an article, also in the *Baltimore Sun,* adopted a somewhat more cautious tone: "If this guy [Neverdon] walks, the thinking went, then it confirms our worst fears about racial divisions in this country. . . . Did the jury deliberating the Joel Lee murder blow it? It sounds like it, and it feeds into a suspicion that nonblacks have about black jurors going easy on black defendants. . . . Joel Lee really was an innocent, and somebody should pay for his death" (Olesker 1995). Several jurors later "ardently" defended the verdict they had reached (James and West 1995).

The Joel Lee murder happened one year after the Los Angeles riots of 1992, when memories of clashes between African American looters and Korean store owners in Los Angeles were still fresh—including the case of Du Soon Ja, a Korean store owner in South Central Los Angeles who shot a fifteen-year-old African American girl, Latasha Harlins, in the back of the head after assuming that she was stealing from her store. That shooting took place in March 1991, and Du's sentencing later that year to five years' probation and community service was met with outrage and often cited as one of the causes of the riots the following year. As the decade drew to a close, it appeared that feelings of interracial animosity remained unresolved across the continent.

Nineteen ninety-seven, the year of my arrival in Baltimore, was a challenging one for Korean entrepreneurs in the city. According to Edward Chang, the rate of business ownership among Koreans is 71 percent higher than their share of the U.S. population, meaning that a clear majority of Koreans in the United States are business (to be precise, small business) owners

(Chang 2003). Baltimore is no exception. According to the 2010 census, while Asians accounted for only 2.3 percent of the city's residents, Asian-owned firms accounted for 5.9 percent of its total of 42,000 firms (U.S. Census Bureau 2012). In 1997, four Korean American merchants were robbed in the city of Baltimore within the space of a mere eight days, two of the assaults resulting in deaths. In relation to a two-man team wearing black ski masks that was involved in at least one of the attacks, a Baltimore police spokesman claimed that such robbers "seem to be extremely violent and don't seem too concerned with getting the money," adding that "Even when they get the money, they become violent anyway" (James 1997). In one attack, a forty-four-year-old Korean grocer and father of three, Chi Sup Kim, was shot twice in the head in front of his wife, having already complied with the robbers' demands by handing over several hundred dollars. Korean merchants in the city feared for their lives, for the safety of their families, and for their financial future, forming the strong impression that the attacks were part of a systemic effort to undermine the local Korean population.

In some other aspects, too, Korean store owners were placed under pressure. For example, in the same year a Korean grocery store was forced to close down for having allegedly sold out-of-date meat. According to my reading of a related article in the *Baltimore Sun*, this incident carried racial undertones. There were ugly scenes at a community meeting held after the closing of the store, including the use of racist slurs, for instance, the deliberate mispronunciation of the name of the store, Canaan Market, as "Canine Market," an allusion to the inclusion of dog meat in the Korean diet (Olesker 1997; see Chapter 3 of this volume). Racial prejudice was undoubtedly one of huge hurdles that Koreans in Baltimore had to overcome, and that had to do not just with the city's African American population. I wrote elsewhere that one of my students at Johns Hopkins was traumatized as a child by white bullies in a nice middle-class Baltimore suburb where she and her family lived (Ryang 2008: chap. 1).

The history of Korean immigration to Baltimore is rather a short one. It was only after the enactment of the Immigration Reform Law in 1965 that the possibility opened up for Koreans to migrate to the United States, leading to a rapid increase in the Korean population. The national pattern was mirrored at city and state levels in Baltimore and Maryland in general. The local Korean Society was founded in 1971, marking the beginning of a wave of migration that would bring tens of thousands of South Koreans to the city (Krimmel 2004). Since 1977, Baltimore's Korean community has held an annual ethnic festival (Madison Park 2007). In 1997, arriving from Australia, changing planes at JFK Airport and boarding a TWA flight bound for Baltimore/Washington International Airport, I already noticed a marked Korean presence, with Koreans accounting for approximately half of the passengers on board. A kind Korean offered me a lift from the airport to a downtown Korean clinic run by the mother of a Korean American friend. My friend's mother, a physician, had generously agreed to put me up for my first few weeks in Baltimore while I waited for my goods to arrive from Australia.

(Re)Discovering *Jeon*

One of the first restaurants in Baltimore I was taken to after moving out of my friend's mother's home into my own apartment was a Korean one. Inviting me were Sidney Mintz, one of the founders of the Department of Anthropology at Johns Hopkins University and recently retired after many decades of service to the field, and his wife Jackie. The restaurant occupied half of the basement level of a corner building in a residential neighborhood. While Sid ordered an eel dish, Jackie chose *bibimbap*. As I looked at the menu, the first thing that came into my mind was *pajeon,* pancake with leeks, *pa* being leeks and *jeon,* pancake. I had sometimes eaten Korean food while living in Australia, where I had been a research fellow in the capital city of Canberra, although there had only been a handful of Korean restaurants in the city in those days (i.e., the mid-1990s). My favorites were *bibimbap* and *kimchijige,* the latter dish a kind of *kimchi* hotpot; but I could not recall having seen *pajeon* at any of the Korean restaurants I had visited in Canberra. So I decided to try this dish when I saw it on the menu of this friendly restaurant in Baltimore. After the usual appetizers and side dishes had been served, followed by *miso* (bean curd) soup, the main dishes arrived. First, I was taken aback by the size of my pancake: it was huge—about twelve inches in diameter. One bite—that unmistakable texture of leeks mixed with oily sesame-seed batter—brought back all sorts of memories of my childhood in Japan.

Growing up among Koreans in Japan during the 1960s, a population that consisted of former colonial immigrants and their descendants, I can attest that food was one of the most important components holding together our shared sense of ethnic identity (Sandra Soo-Jin Lee 2000; see Ryang 1997;

Ryang 2010). Among all of my food-related memories, I recall one event that always involved *jeon*—this was *jesa*, the family ritual in which ancestors are commemorated and honored. Being a traditional ceremonial food, *jeon* would have been served at weddings, on a patriarch's sixtieth birthday, or at any other family celebrations or ceremonial events. By the 1970s, traditional weddings had become increasingly rare, with Koreans in Japan tending to get married in large and upscale Western or Chinese restaurants or, more prestigiously, in hotel banquet rooms where, again, catered food was provided. A *jesa* ceremony was difficult to contract out, however, as it was quintessentially a family event as well as a spiritual ceremony that commercial outlets in Japan would not have been able to comprehend. Such ceremonies formed part of the life cycle for many Koreans in Japan. Standing in the kitchen alongside her mother and her female family elders, a girl would learn how to cook and prepare *jesa* dishes for her natal ancestors; this knowledge and experience later becoming useful when serving her in-laws. A boy would learn how to present and arrange the dishes—in which order and facing which direction (east, west, north, or south) on the altar table. The division of labor had it that women cooked for the ancestors and men presented the food to the ancestors. During her menstrual cycle, a woman had to avoid handling or cooking food.

Jesa-related horror stories abounded among my classmates, many of whom had had arranged marriages. A typical story would involve a new bride being invited to participate in the preparation of food for a *jesa* and turning out to have inferior skills or, worse, being judged utterly incompetent by her female in-laws. Twenty-five years or so later, the roles would shift, with the former bride, no longer young and vulnerable and now a matriarch herself, casting a critical eye over her son's young wife as she made preparations for a *jesa*. This said, it is true that the trend among Koreans in Japan today is for *jesa* no longer to be strictly observed; this ritual now belongs to the bygone world of colonial immigrants, who tried over an extended period, and often in an exaggerated manner, to safeguard practices they had brought from the old motherland. For more than forty years now, since 1973, the number of Koreans in Japan marrying Japanese has exceeded that of those marrying fellow Koreans (Yeong-dal Kim 1996: 179). Thus, the *jesa* is a story of yesteryear.

Not being the eldest son in his family, my father does not bear the duty of observing *jesa*. But this was not the case for a few of our Korean neighbors in the Tokyo suburb where I lived. One family had to perform the ceremony close to twenty times a year, whereas the frequency was lower in other cases. As a child, the reason I knew this was because whenever a Korean family in our neighborhood held a *jesa*, we were bound to receive some of the food from the offerings that had not been consumed by the family. Indeed, judging from the way my Korean neighbors conducted their *jesa*, it appeared that such ceremonies meant, by default, an excess of food. Along with this, my Korean neighbors believed that the generous distribution of ritual food would attract good luck to the distributing family. Among the food items distributed throughout the neighborhood, *jeon* was the most prominent. Sliced into small pieces, these pancakes were easy to wrap and carry around, and the women of the family that had held the *jesa* would simply distribute them among their Korean neighbors. They were stored in the refrigerator and later heated up by being lightly fried in a frying pan with sesame-seed oil—microwave ovens were not yet widely available. Other dishes were either too expensive, and therefore cooked in limited quantities, or contained liquid, making them cumbersome to distribute among neighbors. The portability of *jeon* led to this food being marked as a sign that a *jesa* had taken place in the neighborhood. In such a manner, *jeon,* its portability and the way it circulated around the neighborhood, along with its aroma of sesame-seed oil, became quintessentially associated with *jesa* in my second-generation immigrant child's mind.

The *jesa* is an event based strictly around lineage. Despite my childish imaginings of what might have been taking place in other households, I was unable to attend any *jesa,* as our family did not hold such ceremonies. It was only after becoming an adult that I had opportunities to observe such events—but not to participate in them, as I was an unmarried woman when I was living in Japan. Because of this, I never had the chance to be involved in cooking or serving food at a *jesa,* let alone bowing in ceremonial fashion to the ancestors. While conducting fieldwork for my doctoral research among Koreans in Japan from 1991 to 1992 and then again in 1993 and 1994, I was invited—or allowed, depending on the degree of closeness between myself and the families involved—to be an ethnographic observer at numerous *jesa* held by Koreans in Japan during that time. Come to think of it now, these were the final years in which *jesa* were performed seriously among many Korean families in Japan.

Formal procedure dictates that the dishes for a *jesa* must be prepared in accordance with proscribed rules associated with taboos and preferences, these dishes consisting of the following fourteen items: (1) rice; (2) noodles; (3) sticky rice cakes; (4) three boiled dishes including meat, fish, and vegetables; (5) three meat, fish, or vegetable *jeok* (kebabs); (6) *jeon* (including meat and fish pancakes); (7) *namul* (cooked and seasoned vegetables), and salad-like *kimchi* (using no red chili or salted shrimp); (8) soy sauce; (9) dried fish and shellfish; (10) soup; (11) a variety of fruits of diverse color; (12) sweets made of white sugar; (13) tea cakes; and (14) *sungnyung* (blackened rice mixed with warm water) (Kim and Jeong 2002: 153–154). Items that must not be used for *jesa* include: "hairy" fruits, such as peaches; fish that do not have scales; strong spices, such as chili powder; and vegetables with strong odors, such as garlic and onions. Pig meat should be used instead of horse meat, as horses do not have cloven hooves—an interesting inversion of the rules in Leviticus (Douglas 1966). No dogs should be offered (dog being a traditional meat in Korea). When presenting food, only men should be involved in the final placement of food on the altar table.

Strict rules also apply to the placement of food. For the fourth row of food (i.e., that closest to the audience and therefore farthest from the ancestors), one should offer, from left to right, dates, chestnuts, persimmon, and pears. Cooked and seasoned vegetables *(namul)*, lightly grilled kebab-like skewer dishes *(jeok)*, dried seafood *(po)*, and dessert drinks *(sikhye)* should be placed in the third row of food. The second row should include noodles and rice cakes, while rice, soup, spoons, chopsticks, and wine glasses should be placed in the first row closest to, or right in front of, the ancestors, who are thought to descend and take their designated seats during the ceremony (Kim and Jeong 2002: 153). According to general principles regarding presentation, red fruits are to be placed on the east side, with white fruits on the west; dried foods are to be placed on the left (of the ancestors) and raw and wet foods on the right; plates should be placed on the west side and wine glasses on the east; rice on the right, and soup on the left (Kim and Jeong 2002: 153). No one should eat any of the food before all of the items have been offered to the ancestors (Kim and Jeong 2002: 155). Each altar table should have a designated spot for the ancestors to descend to. Traditionally speaking, *jesa* offerings should occur between 11:00 p.m. and 1:00 a.m., although work and school schedules in modern-day South Korea have led to ceremonies becoming much shorter and taking place earlier in the evening, roughly between 8:00 p.m. and 9:00 p.m. (Kim and Jeong 2002: 149).

Whether or not my Korean neighbors in Japan observed these rules is highly suspect. For example, the *jesa jeon* that I was familiar with while growing up in Japan often contained leeks and chives, despite the fact that leeks, chives, green onions, and onions are considered taboo items due to their strong odor. I even remember *kimchijeon* being used as *jesa* offerings, a practice that would also be against the rules. Koreans in Japan made do with what they had in order to preserve traditions from their homeland. If there were any irregularities, whether due to a lack of knowledge or a result of the sheer impossibility of obtaining traditional Korean ingredients in Japan, these would have been rationalized, one way or another. At any rate, the fact that Koreans in Japan were observing *jesa* in locations removed from their motherland, their ancestral homes, and their family graves already compromised the authenticity of the ceremonies. Seen against this background, the fact that I was eating *jeon,* a ceremonial food used in *jesa* rituals, at a Korean restaurant in Baltimore begins to look extraordinary.

Jeon à la carte

It will be helpful to provide for the reader a brief explanation of how *jeon* are made. Because of the lack of a more appropriate name in English, I will follow conventional cookbooks in using the term "pancakes" when referring to this dish. Nothing about *jeon,* however, resembles the kind of pancakes that Americans might picture, namely, covered in maple syrup, strawberries, and whipped cream. To begin with, *jeon* are not sweet. Ingredients can be divided into those used for the "body" of the pancake—meat, seafood, and vegetables, sometimes precooked and preseasoned (particularly in the case of meat), but often raw (for vegetables or seafood)—and those used for the batter. Korean-language cookbooks refer to batter as *ot* or clothing, and describe the application of the batter using the phrase *osseul ipphida,* meaning to put on clothes or to dress. Neatly trimmed fillets of meat or fish are dipped into batter and shallow-fried, bearing no resemblance whatsoever to cakes. On the other hand, *jeon* containing chopped vegetables and/or sliced seafood, often mixed with green onions and chili, do look like pancakes or, say, flattened frittatas, which, after being panfried, are sliced into appropriately sized pieces.

After acquiring my own apartment and the driver's license that I had never needed in Japan or in England, I began to explore Baltimore. Once, while traveling along a main road that used to be the only route connecting

Baltimore to York, Pennsylvania, I saw a rundown food store that was unmistakably a Korean grocery. The reason I was able to tell this was that my mother used to own a grocery with a very similar frontage. As her store was in Japan, it was a much smaller-scale operation. In Japan, unless one lives in an area with a high density of Korean residents, Korean grocery stores tend to be buried amid mainstream or traditional Japanese stores. This store on the northern outskirts of Baltimore resembled my mother's in that there were angled refrigerators standing right in front of the store, facing the street, and then shelves packed with dried foods, the most conspicuous being huge bundles of dried seaweed. Inside, one refrigerator was filled with small, presumably homemade delicatessen containers. A middle-aged couple ran the store, and when I visited it for the first time, I found the wife sitting in a corner trimming the roots of bean sprouts, a task I had always helped my mother perform.

My father was a college professor, but because of his conscious refusal to have any association with South Korea, then under military rule, he opted to work for a North Korean–influenced university in Japan, meaning that his salary was not sufficient to support our family. This obliged my mother, therefore, to provide for the family, often working twelve-hour shifts running a small Korean grocery store, which eventually became quite successful, financially speaking. As for that little store in Baltimore, I was not sure what kind of future it or its owners were heading for. Although my mother's store was not packed with customers all of the time, curious Japanese passersby or regular customers from the area would frequently come and go. Whenever I visited the store in Baltimore to buy a small jar of *kimchi* or a packet of fishcakes, however, I was always the only customer.

Some months passed; my first year in Baltimore came to an end. In the meantime, my daughter was born prematurely and had to spend time in a neonatal intensive care unit, later being transferred to Johns Hopkins Hospital. Spending all of my time at the hospital with my baby during the next six months, I was in no position to think about Korean food. Once I was able to bring my daughter home, I began eating it again. The first thing that came into my mind was an image of a bundle of dried seaweed. Weren't new mothers supposed to eat seaweed soup? I remembered what my grandmother used to say to my aunts who had just had babies. So, I drove out to that little store.

I could not find it. I drove up and down the street, just in case I had missed it. I thought I might have taken a wrong turn somewhere along the way. After driving around for a while, I gave up. Soon, with my daughter's frequent visits to the hospital and my work commitments, I stopped cooking, becoming increasingly dependent on deli and carry-out foods. Again, I became a frequent visitor to the Korean restaurant where Sid and Jackie had taken me. My favorite to-go item, needless to say, was *jeon,* and my orders would alternate between my three favorite dishes: *gochu pajeon* (*jeon* with hot chili and leeks), *haemul pajeon* (*jeon* with seafood), or the simpler *pajeon* (leek *jeon*). Here again, the portability of this dish made it very convenient.

Into the Suburbs

A few years later, I gave birth to a healthy baby boy. In 2002, we purchased our first family home in the western suburb of Catonsville, Baltimore County, literally across the street from the more affluent Ellicott City, Howard County, where we could not find a home within our budget. It was then that I understood why my little Korean store in Baltimore City had closed down. The home we bought was located between two giant Korean/Asian supermarkets, one in Ellicott City and the other in Catonsville. Now, I no longer needed to pick up carry-out food from restaurants, as the deli sections of both of these stores never ran out of a large variety of delicious Korean food items, including all kinds of *jeon.* Their fresh produce departments had an abundant range of the kinds of fruit and vegetables that I had only ever seen in tiny portions in esoteric corners of conventional American food stores, if at all. Bushels of jujube dates, boxes of mung beans and pine nuts, freezer shelves full of LA *galbi* (sliced short ribs that are great for barbecues), fish eggs, pigs' feet, and so it went on. The large variety of condiments, sauces, oils, seasonings, and snack items they stocked were directly imported from Japan and Korea, many of them bearing brand names that were familiar to me. Both supermarkets had sections selling small- and medium-sized household goods, others featuring Korean-made cosmetics, herbal medicine items, souvenirs, trinkets, and stationery items, and both had comprehensive fresh bakeries. One of them was attached to a food court; the other contained a sit-down eatery.

There were a number of specialized businesses ranged alongside these supermarkets: a Korean bookstore, a store selling traditional Korean furniture, a Korean outfitting and bridal shop, a Korean bedding and mattress store, a video rental shop, Korean-style karaoke bars *(noraebang),* Korean restaurants (including one where diners could enjoy a table-top grill), the office of a Korean-speaking insurance broker, and a tutoring service for Korean children. Thus, although we had moved to Catonsville due to budgetary restraints and the fact that it was located roughly halfway between my place of work and that of my husband, I soon realized that this location offered me significant additional benefits in terms of my access to Korean foods and goods. Returning to the fate of the small Korean grocery store, it was easy to understand why it had closed down; it was simply unable to compete with these large-scale supermarkets, one of which was reported to have had a weekly sales figure of a half-million dollars (Williams 2007).

According to the state census of 2010, Maryland had a Korean population of 45,486 out of a total Asian population of 290,108 (U.S. Census 2010a). As with many other immigrant groups, years of hard work had enabled many Koreans in Baltimore City to relocate to more affluent suburbs. One such suburb with a sizeable Korean population was the Ellicott City area of Howard County. One of the reasons why housing in that area had rapidly become unaffordable for many (including my family) by the early 2000s was due to this very relocation of the Korean population. The influx of Korean families, noted for their intense focus on education, led to a rapid improvement in SAT scores at the local public high school, in turn leading to a significant rise in the price of housing in the area. This would also explain why two large-scale Korean retail outlets emerged in Ellicott City and the adjoining area of Catonsville during the late 1990s and early 2000s. In 2009, Howard County, Maryland, had a population of 282,169 and an average household income of $118,688; its per capita income of $43,133 was $8,284 higher than that of Maryland as a whole (Howard County Maryland Economic Development Authority 2011a). In this county, Ellicott City had 11,148 Asian residents out of a total population of 59,332. This meant that 18.8 percent of the Ellicott City population was Asian, compared to a figure of 5.5 percent for Maryland and a figure of 4.8 percent for the United States as a whole (Howard County Maryland Economic Development Authority 2011b; U.S. Census Bureau 2012). It was also reported that more than 6,000 Koreans were living in Howard County during the early 2000s (Jason Song 2002). In terms of household income, 45 percent of Ellicott City households earned between $100,000 and $249,000 in 2010, a range that is considerably higher than the statewide average (Howard County Maryland Economic Development Authority 2011b).

For Koreans living in this affluent suburb during the first decade of the new millennium, life looked quite different from the bleak reality faced by many Koreans in Baltimore City during the 1990s. Even in Baltimore City itself, Koreans began enjoying a notable increase in visibility, with entrepreneurs beginning to regain confidence. For example, the city's Korean-American Grocers and Licensed Beverage Association (with a membership of 300) held a forum in 2003 exploring how to work more closely with the state attorney's office and the police department. In addition, five Koreans could be found among the two hundred or so prosecutors in the state attorney's office, while at Baltimore District Court, Jeannie Hong became the nation's first female Korean American judge (Neufeld 2003). By the early 2000s, up to a quarter of the entire undergraduate body at the Homewood Campus of Johns Hopkins University, the prestigious institution located right in the heart of the city, was made up of API (Asian and Pacific Islander) students. There was a corresponding boom in Korean video rentals, popular among students (Jason Song 2003). Out in the suburbs, reflecting the influx of Korean residents, English-language classes for new immigrants enjoyed a period of explosive growth, while a Korean community organization in Howard County launched a Care Line to provide recent Korean immigrants with useful information to help them adjust to their new lives in the United States (Morgan 2002; O'Grady 2003). Although the shocking shooting rampage in nearby Virginia by a Korean American student at Virginia Tech in 2007 led Koreans to be more vigilant, even forcing some to overcompensate by trying to exhibit good behavior, the fact that this incident did not result in a major backlash against the Korean community led Koreans in the area to breathe a collective sigh of relief (Brewington 2007).

When I visited the western suburbs of Baltimore, spending the summer of 2011 there as part of my fieldwork activities and frequenting both of its large supermarkets, I noticed that employees were wary of talking to me. In the past, when I had lived in Catonsville, the *ajumma* (middle-aged women) working at these supermarkets had always been happy to tell me their stories and explain the ingredients that went into the large jars of *kimchi* that they were putting out on display. In 2011, however, not only did they remain silent, but they also made excessive efforts to avoid me or anyone else who tried to talk to them. American customers who were initially curious about certain items in the store would ask a few questions and then give up after a few attempts, most likely assuming that the store employees did not understand English. But even when I tried talking to them in

Korean, they would refuse to talk to me. Later, after reading a few newspaper articles, I was able to figure out that the reticence of the staff was part of a concerted effort on the part of both stores not to verbally give out any information. This was not due to any kind of rivalry between the two, but to the negative publicity that had followed a controversial inspection of one of the stores in 2007. The store was accused of violating hygiene standards and was temporarily shut down. Even though the newspaper article had quoted some worrying data related to hygiene standards there, the store appeared to be thriving just as it had always done when I visited it in 2011 (Carson 2007). Whenever I shopped in this store, I found it full of a diverse range of customers, reflecting its unbeatable prices and the freshness of its produce. As far as I could tell, both stores demonstrated an almost excessive adherence to flawless standards of cleanliness and hygiene, perhaps in response to the 2007 incident.

The deli counter at one of these stores featured packets of *jeon* lined up and ready for easy collection. Particularly appetizing among them was a variety pack containing meat, fish, onion, and chili *jeon*. Each packet included a dainty plastic container of dipping sauce. In themselves, the packages exhibited a colorful air of festivity. How strange—I thought—to see *jesabanchan* (side dishes of *jesa*) at a Korean supermarket in a Maryland suburb. Compared to the colonial-immigrant version of *jeon* in Tokyo, cooked as a ritual offering for ancestors in a faraway homeland, this version, arranged in variety packs in a large supermarket, had entirely lost its ritual meaning. No longer offered to the ancestors, and with no regard paid to the rules associated with the placement of foods at a proper *jesa* ritual, this *jeon* would find itself prosaically placed on a plate and served as a side dish at a family dinner or eaten as a quick lunch. Were these *jeon,* then, not being offered for anything at all? The admittedly somewhat ironic answer would have to be that they were being offered in celebration of the tireless entrepreneurship of Korean Americans who had turned this sacred object into a secular, commercial product. Whether in the form of slices of *jesa-jeon* distributed throughout Korean ethnic neighborhoods in Japan or as variety packs of *jeon* sold at Baltimore's Asian supermarkets, both bore, to varying degrees but nonetheless present, metonymic fragments of colonialism, immigration, and diaspora.

One could not help noticing the resilience shown by local Korean merchants over the years, particularly in the wake of violent attacks that had claimed the lives of some of their own in the mid-1990s. Once transnational

Asian-American capital advanced to the suburbs in the wake of the new millennium, however, the city's small Korean grocery stores started going out of business, one by one. Indeed, it was not some external, non-Korean or anti-Korean force that pushed them out of business, but rather the arrival of larger Korean and Asian food stores that presented themselves as one-stop shops, not only for a diverse range of food items, but also for traditional clothing, household utensils, furniture, books, and cosmetics. This, too, is an example of the reality of globalization and global capitalism, and a very ironic one at that.

The Korean Table

In somewhat of a departure from the celebratory notion of ethnic food in the United States portrayed by Donna Gabaccia (1998), Ji-Yeon Yuh asserts that "food fights" or a domestic clash of tastes between different cultures continue to occur between Korean food and American food in the context of the diet and cooking practices of Korean military brides (Yuh 2002: 127). Yuh further notes that this clash does not simply derive from differences in tastes, but also from the different structures of each cuisine: whereas American meals are usually structured around the formula of one main dish accompanied by two side dishes—following Mary Douglas (1972)—Korean meals are structured "around a bowl of rice and several side dishes" and "everything is served at once" (Yuh 2002: 144). I would add, however, that everything is not always served at once. Often, when entertaining dinner guests, one first serves liqueurs and wines *(sul)*, accompanied by *anju*, little sides for drinks, which Marja Vongerichten calls "the name for food that accompanies drinks" (Vongerichten 2011: 204).

As insignificant as this may sound, one notices that one can find no equivalent to *anju* in the American diet or drinking culture. When encountered at one of the little drinking tents or covered stalls in the markets of Seoul, *anju* may include items such as skewered meat and seafood, dumplings, grilled meat and vegetables, dried fish, barbecued shrimp, pigs' feet, fish cakes, and so on. In a home environment, it might include finger food such as dried calamari or spicy fish or, more frequently, small portions of vegetables, tofu, fish and/or meat, as well as *kimchi*—that is to say, the kind of dishes one would normally find at a regular dinner. Structurally speaking, wine and *anju* constitute integral parts of the evening meal. Typically in such a case, *sul* and *anju* are followed by a bowl of rice and soup to finish off the meal. In this way, drinks served with small portions of side dishes slide into dinner. Clearly, the rice and soup follow the *sul* and *anju* and are not all presented at once. Likewise, the Korean traditional dessert *(husik)*—for example, the thick and sweet rice drink called *sikhye*—necessarily comes after all the other dishes have been eaten and so is not served at the same time as everything else. The term *husik* itself consists of the Chinese characters *hu,* meaning "after," and *sik,* meaning "meal."

Yuh's description, however, does capture the essence of the practices associated with the serving of Korean food in that Korean meals do not necessarily include a main dish, as in the standard "meat-and-two-vegetables" style common to dinner tables in Anglophone households, or a series of courses, as found in French cuisine, tending instead to include many dishes that are served together. Traditionally, the wealthier the family doing the entertaining, the larger was the number of dishes served, rising in odd-number increments from three to five and then seven, with the king at the apex of the system eating a twenty-seven-dish meal five times a day (see Introduction). Likewise, the higher the status of the guest, the larger was the number of dishes offered. In this manner of serving, out of three, five, or seven dishes, no one was deemed to be the main dish, all of them having more or less equal standing on the table.

In Korea today and also in Koreatowns throughout the United States, one can find restaurant menus containing the word *jeongsik.* This term originates from the Japanese term *teishoku,* which is written using the Chinese characters *tei* (to set) and *shoku* (to eat). As is the case for many other food terms that Koreans believe to be their own, including *tonkasseu* (pork fillet) or *udong* (*udon* noodles), this term reflects colonial contact between Japanese and Koreans. (Incidentally, the original Japanese term *tonkatsu* is also a bastardized combination of the Chinese character denoting pork or pig *[ton]* with part of the transliterated English word cutlet *[katsu],* reflecting early Japanese contact with the West in the late-nineteenth century.) Typically, the term *jeongsik* is added to the name of the main dish featured in a particular set meal, such as grilled fish or barbecued meat: examples might include *chamchi jeongsik* (a tuna meal) or *sundubu jeongsik* (a spicy tofu hotpot set). While not all Korean restaurants use this term, the concept of *jeongsik* helps when trying to understand how Korean meals are Americanized and packaged after their arrival in the United States, a process that then boomerangs back to Korea, albeit with a degree of further modification.

A good example of a set meal menu is *bossam,* a barbecued pork wrap that is served at relatively high-end restaurants in Seoul (see color plates). The term *ssam* is used to refer to a wrap. Pork slices are subtly marinated and may be served with spicy carrot salad and oysters, all wrapped in a green-leafed vegetable. One may also wrap a small portion of chopped green chili or indeed any items from the side dishes according to one's tastes. In such a serving, the pork cannot be considered to be the main dish, as any of the side dishes can also be wrapped and eaten in the same way as pork. But one does not get the wrapping leaves or all of the other side dishes unless one orders *bossam.* Here, a new hierarchy is introduced to the table: the other dishes are subordinate to the pork. This goes against traditional Korean table practices, where all of the dishes, the soup, and the rice played more or less equally important and mutually dependent roles.

In this light, the reader will be able to see how strange, even outright ridiculous, it is to serve a bowl of *miso* soup as an appetizer, a common practice at Korean (or Japanese) restaurants in the United States. The Asian-background tasters whom I worked with unanimously reported feeling uncomfortable having to eat soup on an empty stomach—one needed rice with it, they all claimed. Furthermore, rice is not subordinate to anything, traditionally speaking. In Korea, close friends might ask each other early in the afternoon, *"Bap meogeosseo?"* or "Have you had *bap?"* *Bap* is a term that refers to boiled or cooked rice, but here, the appropriate translation would be "Have you had lunch?" rather than "Have you had (cooked or boiled) rice?" For, in Korean, *bap* also refers to a meal—any meal (Kwang Ok Kim 2010). A similar example exists in other parts of the world, including Japan, where *"Gohan tabeta"* would mean "I've eaten a meal," while *gohan*'s proper translation (out of context) would be boiled or cooked rice.

The reader will have begun to see that to have *jeon* as a main dish makes no sense as far as the traditional Korean table is concerned because it is quintessentially a side dish—one of three, five, seven, or even twenty-seven in the case of the Korean kings—and therefore cannot be a main one. By the same token, *jeon* cannot be a side dish either, because, quite practically, no such distinction is made between main and side dishes on the Korean table. But, the Americanized packaging of *jeon* in restaurants means that diners are presented with anomalously huge servings of it—as was the case when I was served a twelve-inch *jeon* in Baltimore—along with rice and some *kimchi,* now called "side dishes," all of them brought out after the soup, which was offered as an appetizer. Nothing could be stranger if one compares such practices with the Korean conventions associated with the serving of meals. The way in which Korean restaurant menus are put together in the United States, therefore, constitutes an egregious compromise involving a drastic modification of traditional Korean food-serving practices. The small plates of appetizers that precede the so-called main dish at standard Korean restaurants throughout the United States are a corrupted version of traditional Korean three-, five-, or seven-dish meals.

The example of *bossam* discussed here comes from Korea, not the United States. One can appreciate that the Korean restaurant business has now fully adapted itself to American-style main-dish-oriented menus, having already adapted to the Japanese *teishoku* (set meal) format during colonial times, itself perhaps a reflection of the influence of Western dining practices on the Japanese themselves. One difference I have noticed is that no restaurant I have dined at in Korea served soup as an appetizer—it always came together with rice. So, where can we witness an authentic Korean meal being served if even in Korea itself meal formats have been Westernized? Basically, nowhere, if we insist on a traditional three-, five-, or seven-dish setting. But the question is: Does authenticity mean primordial, old, original, or traditional? The problem is that none of these attributes are absolute in nature—they are relational attributes, depending on what standards of measurement are applied. One may, for example, talk about a new tradition or an original copy. At a glance, such expressions do not make sense, yet neither is each an oxymoron—they do make sense if we admit that any given thing had to be new at first in order to become old, or that the first copy is the original itself despite the fact that it is also a copy. If authenticity implies the replication of an original recipe, then we have to assume that this original still exists somewhere. But, of course, the act of cooking itself already falls firmly within the realm of reproduction. No one, not even a super-chef, can cook exactly the same dish twice, rendering the act of cooking, strictly speaking, a form of mimicking. This argument has an interesting effect on our discussion of authenticity, which I shall return to in the Conclusion.

3 | Two Colonizations and Three Migrations

Grilling *Galbi*

Precolonial Immigrants

When thinking about Korean immigration to the United States, one cannot avoid talking about Hawai'i, a state in which 40 percent of the population identifies as Asian, not only because it was the first place in the United States on which Korean immigrants set foot, but also because of its multicultural tradition, removed as it is from the U.S. mainland. Koreans migrated to Hawai'i before Korea formally became a Japanese colony. The precolonial aspect of Korean migration to Hawai'i is crucial to understanding the unique attributes of the Korean food found on the islands. Most of the Koreans in Los Angeles, Baltimore, and other areas of the United States arrived after the passing of the 1965 Immigration and Nationality Act, which saw the abolition of the national quota system, and Koreans eventually came to rank among the top five groups of migrants to the United States after 1975. In other words, most Korean immigrants came here after Japan's colonial rule had come to an end (1945), after national partition (1948), and after the end of the civil war (1953). By contrast, the 7,500 Koreans who came to Hawai'i during the years 1903 through 1905 were precolonial immigrants, arriving in Hawai'i several years before Japan formally annexed Korea in 1910. But, unlike the first Japanese migrants to Hawai'i, these Koreans arrived six years after the archipelago had been annexed by the United States (in 1898). According to Wayne Patterson, the very first group of Koreans arriving in Hawai'i at the port of

Honolulu included fifty-six men, twenty-one women, and twenty-five children (Patterson 2000: 1). Precolonial immigration to Hawai'i predominantly revolved around meeting the demand for labor in the archipelago's sugar plantations.

The 1903 immigrants included the grandmother of Elaine Kim, a prominent ethnic studies scholar and activist. Kim writes about her grandmother's arrival in Hawai'i:

> When I was growing up, I heard a lot about my father's history, but no one said much about my mother's background. I figure that my maternal grandmother, a country woman, fled Korea to Hawaii, pregnant and alone around 1903. My mother looked like a person of mixed racial heritage. Could the father she never knew be one of the Russian soldiers who was sent to the Korean peninsula around the time of the Russo-Japanese War? Was my grandmother seduced? Was she raped? Perhaps she considered jumping into a well . . . but was saved by the tiny window of opportunity opened when the Hawaii Sugar Plantation association recruited briefly in Korea to counter the efforts of Japanese sugar workers in Hawaii. . . . (Elaine Kim 1996: 355–356)

Unlike the later forced recruitment of Koreans by the Japanese military government during World War II and their transfer to Japan and beyond as a wartime labor force (including the so-called comfort women), these plantation workers came to Hawai'i—and I use this word with caution—voluntarily. According to Patterson, the mastermind behind this plan, under which Koreans were able to migrate to Hawai'i during a two-and-a-half-year period commencing in 1903, was Horace Allen, the American Minister for Korea. This plan was later thwarted by the Japanese government as Japan's influence grew stronger in Korea in the early twentieth century, the former eventually annexing the latter; the Japanese colonial authorities in Korea considered that an increased Korean presence in Hawai'i would have a compromising effect on its colonization of Korea and undermine Japanese migration to Hawai'i (Patterson 2000: 2–3). Interestingly, Patterson emphasizes that while Japanese immigrants to Hawai'i tended to come from rural areas of southwestern Japanese prefectures and were therefore used to working in agricultural settings, Korean immigrants tended to come from urban areas of the peninsula, were mostly better educated than their Chinese or Japanese counterparts, and were Christian (Patterson 2000: chap. 2). Thus, they did not make a very good plantation workforce, and tried to leave Hawaiʻi for the mainland as soon as they were able to get ahead financially.

Still, once in the islands, the Koreans had to adapt to the plantation lifestyle, their daily lives being largely confined to the fields and the Korean camp. One can only imagine the many shocks they suffered: dress codes, dietary traditions, and other familiar practices, such as those involving gender segregation, needed to be drastically modified or abandoned completely. They would have seen tropical fruits such as pineapples, bananas, and passion fruit for the first time in their lives. Apart from those who had grown up on the southern island of Jeju, they would not have seen oranges before either. The trees were different, the grasses were different, and the soil consisted of volcanic gravel. I wonder whether they stood on beaches, facing in the direction of Korea, reminiscing about their homeland while at the same time marveling at the warm breezes and the sweet smell of tropical flowers of their new home.

In 1905, Koreans accounted for 11 percent of plantation workers, putting them in second place far behind the Japanese at 66 percent (Patterson 2000: 11). According to the U.S. Census of 2000, 16.7 percent of the total state population of Hawaiʻi of about 1.2 million was Japanese and 1.9 percent Korean. Meanwhile, Asians as a whole made up 41.6 percent of the entire population, with whites accounting for 39.3 percent ("Demographic Statistics: Hawaii" 2000). Although there is a strong Asian presence in the archipelago when compared with other parts of the United States, Koreans still form a much smaller proportion of the population than Japanese, paralleling the 1905 statistics for plantation workers already noted. My travels throughout Hawaiʻi led me to discover a pattern that reflected the disparity in population sizes between the Japanese and Korean communities, with the relative Japanese dominance reflecting not only evolving historical conditions but also traces of past colonial relations in intriguing ways. I also discovered an interesting triangular cultural nexus between American, Japanese, and Korean foods.

Scenes of Immigration

If the Koreans who came to Hawaiʻi at the very beginning of the twentieth century can be thought of as precolonial, the Japanese arriving in the archipelago can be considered as pre-annexation—that is, they arrived prior to Hawai'i's annexation by the United States. About 150 Japanese arrived in Hawai'i as contract laborers during 1868, immediately after the restoration of the Meiji emperor of Japan. Statistics relating to the exact number of arrivals vary slightly: Dorothy Ochiai Hazama and Jane Okamoto Komeiji claim a figure of 153; John Van Sant proposes 148 (Hazama and Komeiji 1986: 7; Van Sant 2000: 107). Referred to as *gannenmono*, a term reflecting the fact that they arrived during the first year *(gannen)* of the Meiji era, they became Honolulu's first ever official labor migrants. The work conditions they were subjected to were terrible—bordering on slavery—with Hawai'i's Masters and Servants Act of 1850 stipulating that contracts could last up to five years and authorizing severe punishment for those who violated such contracts (Van Sant 2000: 109).

Following its unification under the great King Kamehameha in 1810, and excluding a five-month period of British occupation in 1843, Hawai'i functioned as an independent kingdom for most of the nineteenth century, right up until its annexation by the United States in 1898. In prior centuries, however, the various islands of the archipelago had been home to a range of separate communities that were deeply religious, observed strict taboos, and were organized in a hierarchical fashion. Western advances on the islands predated unification, with Captain James Cook making visits in 1778 and 1779. By the time Hawai'i's last monarch, Queen Lili'uokalani, was deposed by descendants of American missionaries in 1893, there was an unmistakable level of U.S. economic and military interest in the islands. In the summer of 1898, when the archipelago was annexed by the United States, members of the Hawaiian royal family wore black clothing in order to mark the occasion as the death of the island kingdom (Siler 2012: 286–287). Despite repeated attempts by the former queen at restoring Hawaiian sovereignty, including the publication of memoirs that included a painful plea, Hawai'i formally became a U.S. territory in 1900 (Lili'uokalani 1898; Allen 1982: 370ff.).

Early Japanese migration to Hawai'i took place during the same period as that in which the above events were unfolding. Western interest in the potential of the archipelago for sugar production intensified during the latter part of the nineteenth century. By the 1870s, plantations were in dire need of workers, and they turned to China and Japan to meet this need. In 1885, the first Japanese laborers since the *gannenmono* seventeen years earlier disembarked in Honolulu, four years after the visit to Japan by the Hawaiian king, David Kalākaua (Coffman 2009: 189–190). February 1885 saw the arrival of 945 labor immigrants *(kanyakuimin)*, followed by 983 more in June 1885 (Hazama and Komeiji 1986: 16). As already noted, pre-annexation plantation labor was basically indentured labor, with workers subjected to inhumane work conditions under contracts binding them to several years' labor with no option to terminate or modify their agreements. Despite this state of affairs, the government of Japan, itself a newly emerged political entity, sent warships to the archipelago in 1897 in a show of support for the Hawaiian monarchy, which had just been overthrown by a group of American businessmen and lawyers who were the descendants of missionaries in Hawai'i.

Behind this move lay the issue of the deprivation of political rights of Japanese workers in Hawai'i; in 1887, prior to its annexation, the kingdom was forced by the armed Americans to adopt a new constitution, referred to as the Bayonet Constitution, which denied non-Hawaiians voting rights. As mentioned, by the time the first Korean immigrants arrived in Hawai'i in the early years of the twentieth century, Japanese workers accounted for the largest proportion of the sugar plantation labor force. Due to anti-Japanese feeling following the archipelago's annexation, Japanese workers and their families and descendants in Hawai'i were forced to carve out their own politico-cultural space at their own expense. Japanese schools were established during the period from the 1890s through the early 1900s, the curriculum modeled on the one used in schools in Japan (including language and moral education) and using textbooks approved by the Japanese Ministry of Education (Hazama and Komeiji 1986: 84). By 1910, over seven thousand students were enrolled at 140 Japanese-language schools throughout the archipelago, the number doubling to fourteen thousand by 1916 (Kimura 1988: 186). By 1934, a total of 183 schools were teaching more than 41,000 Japanese students their language, history, and culture (Takagi 1987). By the 1930s, many second-generation Japanese had learned a sufficient amount of Japanese to enter professions that required proficiency in Japanese as well as English (Odo 2004: 60). The total population of Hawai'i in 1910 was 191,909, a figure that included 79,675 Japanese (twenty thousand of whom were U.S. citizens). By 1920, the Japanese population had jumped to 109,274, this figure including fifty thousand naturalized citizens (Kimura 1988: 186). Japanese immigration continued until the passing by the U.S. Congress of the Japanese Exclusion Act in 1924, which completely prohibited Japanese from migrating to the United States (Kimura 1988: 15).

It is ironic, then, to recall that while the Japanese in Hawai'i were witnessing the loss of Hawaiian sovereignty as a result of pressure from foreign economic and political interests, and were also fighting to preserve their
own cultural integrity in a foreign land, Korea was losing its sovereignty to
Japan, and its people facing their own struggle to maintain their culture
and rights. Indeed, the succession of events on the Korean Peninsula during the late nineteenth century and early twentieth century bears a parallel alignment to events taking place across the Pacific Ocean in Hawai'i.

Japanese advancement in Korea in modern times can be traced back at
least as far as the 1876 open-ports treaty referred to as the Ganghwa Treaty,
while the 1894–1895 Sino-Japanese War was fought on Korean soil. In 1905,
Korea became a Japanese protectorate, its monarch deposed, with the peninsula ultimately annexed by Japan in 1910. After Korea became a Japanese
colony, the Japanese colonial administration that was established in Seoul
prohibited Koreans from migrating to Hawai'i or other parts of the United
States. At the same time, a land survey and other administrative reforms
deprived Koreans of their jobs, property, and rights, forcing many into des-
titution and pushing many others to migrate north to China in search of
farmland and south to Japan, the colonial metropolis, in search of work and
better living standards. Just as in the case of the Japanese population in
Hawai'i, there was a steady increase in the number of Koreans in Japan.
And just like the Japanese who migrated to Hawai'i, at least initially, most
Korean immigrants to Japan were single male workers. By the 1930s, however, many had started families and settled in Japan. About 300,000 Koreans were living in Japan by 1930, the figure rising to 600,000 in 1935, 1.2
million in 1940, and then to 2.1 million in 1945, the year in which World
War II came to an end (Morita 1996). Like the Japanese in Hawai'i, Koreans in Japan were deprived of their civil and political rights. The majority
were day laborers, low-wage workers, and small business owners eking out
a meager existence. Just as the Japanese in Hawai'i had to deal with prejudice and discrimination, so Koreans in Japan also faced prejudice and discrimination from the Japanese, many of whom viewed the Koreans as
ignorant, backward, and inferior to them.

My fieldwork in Hawai'i was underscored by overlapping histories of
migration and colonialism—one involving the emigration of Japanese to
Hawai'i, and the other the emigration of Koreans to Japan. Unlike the Japanese in Hawai'i, who had grown in number to exceed 200,000, or 16.8

percent of the "one race" category in the 2000 U.S. census, Koreans accounted for only 23,530, or 1.9 percent of Hawai'i's population, reflecting the fact that the early Korean migrants to Hawai'i did not stay on the islands, but moved to the mainland when the opportunity arose ("Demographic Statistics: Hawaii" 2000). These figures contrast markedly with those for ethnic populations in the United States as a whole. According to the same 2010 census data, the total Korean population in the United States was 1,463,474, an increase of 33 percent over the 2000 figure of 1,099,422, while the total Japanese population declined from 852,237 in 2000 to 841,824 in 2010 (Hoeffel et al. 2012). As I set out on my fieldwork in Hawai'i, my primary goal was to find a bridge linking Korea and Hawai'i via the continuing strong Japanese presence on the island.

Looking for *Galbi*

The Hawai'i I first visited was some distance from Honolulu, the port where those first Korean migrants had landed. I opted to base myself mainly in Kona and, to some extent, Hilo, on the island of Hawai'i, more commonly known as the Big Island. My decision was based on my desire to recapture a more traditional Hawai'i regardless of the obvious limitations of such a strategy, one that was removed from the forces of global capital and the dense urban environment of Honolulu, which I visited on my second fieldtrip to Hawai'i. In Kona, the birthplace of King Kamehameha carries historical memories of the loss of the Kingdom of Hawai'i to the United States, whereas Queen Lili'uokalani Gardens in Hilo commemorates Japanese immigration and traditional Japanese gardening culture while at the same time paying tribute to the last queen of the Kingdom of Hawai'i.

Unlike Honolulu, Kona has been somewhat off the radar for the intense waves of globalization, having only recently begun to develop a local tourist industry. According to the 2010 U.S. census, 36.7 percent of Kona's total population of 11,975 was white and 18.1 percent Asian. These proportions differed considerably from those for Hawai'i as a whole, where 24.7 percent of the 2010 population of 1.36 million was white and 38.6 percent Asian. In the same year, while 47.2 percent of firms in Hawai'i as a whole were Asian-owned, the figure for Kona was only 21.4 percent (U.S. Census Bureau 2010b, using figure for Kailua-Kona). However, there was a conspicuous Japanese presence in Kona, with Japanese restaurants to be found not only in tourist areas, with their high-end menus and pricing, but in local neighborhoods as well. A few nostalgic-looking noodle houses and *shokudō*, Japanese-style eateries, beckoned to me as I drove along a narrow ridge on Highway 11 in the direction of Kīlauea volcano where, according to native legend, the Hawaiian goddess Pele resides. Despite the relative remoteness of this region, it was still easy to find signs of a long history of Japanese immigration there.

In Kona, even a Super Target store had a large Asian food aisle offering not only obvious items such as instant noodles and shrimp-flavored crackers, but also more specialized ones such as dried squid, Japanese rice cakes, and imported packets of *tsukemono,* Japanese pickled vegetables. There were also locally owned Japanese supermarkets in Kona clearly bearing Japanese family names in their logos. In one such store, a large deli section included a dozen or so shelves filled with a diverse range of Japanese ready-to-eat items in small plastic containers. Interestingly, these items were labeled with names that mixed Hawaiian and Japanese words. For example, a *tako poke* was a raw octopus salad, the term being a fusion of *tako,* the Japanese word for octopus, and *poke,* the Hawaiian word for a raw fish salad typically mixed with sea salt, soy sauce, sesame oil, and Maui onions (sliced and chopped), with or without diced tomato. The unmistakable similarity in syllabic structure between the Japanese and Polynesian/Hawaiian languages allowed them to work together in perfect harmony, producing a delightfully rhythmic refrain of vowels accentuated by lyrical consonant sounds.

The assortment of deli items found at one Japanese supermarket that I visited included seaweed salad and chopped squid salad (see color plates). Such items can also be found in the Korean food inventory. When one tastes them, they reveal their Japaneseness, so to say, as they lack garlic, sesame seed oil and, most important, the smoky, musty flavor of red chili powder present in Korean seaweed or squid salad. In short, these deli items have a subtler flavoring than that of comparable Korean deli items. I soon realized that this assortment of deli dishes constituted a microcosm of the way in which Korean food existed in Kona—that is to say, embedded in other foods.

In Kona, Korean restaurants and grocery stores seemed to be conspicuously absent. Although I eventually managed to find one or two Korean restaurants in more locally oriented shopping areas such as strip malls, I came across none in the high-end, touristy areas of Kona. I was intrigued by one restaurant I visited in a low-key strip mall. The place did not seem anything like the Korean restaurants in the U.S. mainland that I had gotten used to, with their large menus and, above all, their Korean servers. Here, one ordered one's main dish from the woman across the counter, who would then let one choose from the assortment of side dishes laid out under glass. I picked potato noodle salad or *japchae, kimchi,* and bean sprouts for my *galbi* barbecued beef, in addition to *bibimbap.* After five minutes or so, my food came out of a little square opening on the wall that completely covered the kitchen area so as not to allow the customers to look and see how food was prepared, rendering the cooking altogether mysterious. A blond woman picked it up and passed it to me.

I was confused, because the food did not have any of the particularly Korean flavoring that one would expect. The seaweed was too sweet, just like Japanese seaweed salad, while the potato noodles simply had a flavor of soy sauce that I would, again, characterize as Japanese rather than Korean. Furthermore, the *galbi* meat came in a big chunk, necessitating the use of a knife and fork—certainly an unconventional form of presentation.

Nevertheless, the place was very popular, its customers drawn from the culturally and ethnically diverse local population and including at least one large, three-generational Korean family, the members of which were chatting to each other in Korean. A Caucasian man sitting next to me at an outdoor table said to me in a friendly manner, "We all love Korean food, don't we?" I smiled, but did not know how to answer because I did not feel that the food was particularly Korean. Then, a question came into my mind: "Why do I feel this way?" This question is associated with my own conception of Korean food as the bearer of a certain taste. Needless to say, this is a question relating to authenticity—the subject of this book. At least one thing seemed to be clear, however. In Kona, Koreans did not have exclusive ownership of Korean food. While bearing the name Korean, this food had been adapted to please the local Hawaiian (read: multicultural) population. In other words, it appeared that Korean food had deviated from its national culinary identity while still being understood as Korean by the locals.

The following day, somehow disappointed by the absence of the taste that I was accustomed to calling Korean—a taste involving chili and garlic, pungent and fermented flavors in addition to, shall we say, some kind of kick to the palate and then to the stomach—I wandered into a Vietnamese restaurant. As I was ordering some *pho* noodle soup, the words "*galbi* barbecue" caught my eye, prompting me to also request *galbi,* just for the sake of trying out their version of this Korean dish. I was surprised when the dish arrived, as this version of *galbi,* served in a Vietnamese restaurant, had a more authentic, or should I say conventional, *galbi* smell. Putting the meat into my mouth, I thought to myself that this place could pass for a Korean restaurant. Yet my Vietnamese *pho* was as authentic (pace the term's ambiguity) as it could have been.

My Vietnamese palate was Australian-trained, and this *pho* was as good as the ones I had enjoyed at Vietnamese restaurants in Sydney and Canberra, typically operated by Vietnamese immigrants. My sense of confusion was only to worsen: many menus of the next few Asian restaurants I checked in the following week contained some kind of Korean barbecue item. Not one of these establishments, however, called itself a Korean restaurant. In addition, the Korean food items that I encountered at some of these restaurants had been creatively Americanized, one restaurant modifying the spelling of *bibimbap* to *bibim*Bob.

After a few weeks in Kona, I drove to Hilo, by now determined to find a Korean restaurant—more specifically, a plate of Korean-tasting *galbi*. I had found one on the Internet that, tellingly, listed *galbi* along with burgers on its menu. It was a Wednesday, the day of Hilo's weekly farmers' market. Dozens of tents had been pitched on the somewhat rustic, old-fashioned, and friendly town square, with stalls selling fruits and vegetables as well as arts and crafts. One stall was stocked with lots of jade and coral items from China, while others featured items such as Indonesian wood carvings, Hawaiian print scarves (mostly made in China), and Japanese and Hawaiian antiques. At some of the stalls, local artists were selling their own creations, one even featuring hand-crafted jewelry made from real Hawaiian native flowers. The craftsman at this stall was an Englishman who happened to be a graduate of the same university that I had gone to, and we found ourselves reminiscing about England while standing in the farmers' market in Hilo, an altogether unexpected development.

None of the stalls, however, included any Korean items. As I weaved my way among the tents, stopping here and there to purchase items such as tangerines and tomatoes, I realized that the streets on the outskirts of the market were lined with a diverse range of ethnic restaurants: Malaysian, Filipino, Mexican, Colombian, Italian, Japanese, and Chinese. There were no Korean restaurants here, either. I was not disappointed, though, as I knew that the Korean restaurant I had found on the Internet was not located in this area. After having driven for close to three hours from Kona, I was feeling hungry. Resisting with all my willpower the urge to eat at one of the restaurants near the market, particularly the Malaysian one, I got back in my car and set off to locate my Korean restaurant. I kept on driving, up and down the street mentioned on the Internet, but was unable to find the restaurant. In the end, I asked some pedestrians where I could find it, only to be told that it had recently gone out of business. Coming to the conclusion that I was not going to find a Korean restaurant serving *galbi* in Hilo, I drove off toward the Queen Lili'uokalani Gardens.

As I drove through these breathtakingly beautiful gardens, I came across a Japanese restaurant built on magnificent stilts, no doubt a tsunami-proof design. Since I had been unable to find any *galbi,* I thought I would enjoy Kobe beef instead. Occupying an outstandingly lovely spot overlooking the gardens, the restaurant was very stylish. Despite the fact that there were many empty tables in its spacious and tastefully decorated interior, I was told that all of the tables had already been booked for a big function that evening, and also that this restaurant normally required advance reservations to be made due to its popularity. I had to grin, for I felt that I was witnessing a palimpsest of colonial history seeping into Hilo's contemporary food scene. Of course, in itself, the fact that an expensive Japanese restaurant occupied one of the most beautiful spots in Hilo did not say much about Korea's colonial history. Rather, it spoke of the long-term relationship between Hawai'i and Japan. Yet in its shadow lay the colonial history of Korea.

In Kona, Korean food is offered in unison or fusion with other foods—whether served at the Vietnamese restaurant that I visited in Kona, for example, or alongside burgers at the Korean restaurant that had gone out of business in Hilo. This pattern contrasts with the impressive Japanese presence in the high-end quarters of both Kona and Hilo as well as with the many informal neighborhood noodle houses and *shokudō.* The latter unequivocally claim to be authentic in that they do not carry any label other than Japanese. Korean food, on the other hand, appears in unexpected or non-national contexts, as my experiences in Kona have shown. I hope it is clear to the reader that I am not implying that one is superior and the other inferior. Rather, I am simply claiming that Korean food is invisible in Kona when compared to the high visibility of Japanese food. Importantly, in my view, there is an interesting parallel, or to be precise an inversion, to be uncovered if one compares the way in which Korean food is made invisible in Kona and the way in which a particular food item becomes Korean in Japan. In order to substantiate my point, I'll have to take a long detour, inviting the reader to Japan and offering a glimpse into another example of colonial history—that of Japan's colonial rule of Korea and of Korean migration to Japan, explored within the context of meat consumption patterns and practices.

Eating Meat in Japan and Korea

Today, half of the world's pork is consumed in China, with China's annual meat consumption skyrocketing from 3.6 kg per person in 1961 to 52.4 kg per person in 2002. In 1961, each Japanese consumed an average of 7.6 kg of meat, the figure increasing to 43.9 kg by 2002; in Korea, the figures were 4.3 kg for 1961 and 48 kg for 2002 (Brown 2009). During the same period, meat consumption in the UK remained remarkably stable, with figures of 69.8 kg and 79.6 kg for 1961 and 2002 respectively, while the corresponding figures for the United States rose from 89.2 kg to 124.8 kg, and those for Denmark from 56.7 kg to 145.9 kg (Brown 2009). From these statistics it can be concluded that Asian nations have experienced a far greater increase in meat consumption than many other nations, with Japan recording a sixfold increase and Korea an impressive tenfold one between the years 1961 and 2002. This dietary shift has been reflected in health-related statistics. Already in 1987, for example, a study recorded a rapid increase in breast cancer among Japanese women due to an increase in the consumption of meat, especially grilled meat, which produces a high proportion of the cancer-causing compounds known as HCAs (Hirayama 1987). Still, it is clear that Europeans and North Americans continue to consume altogether much larger amounts of meat than Asians do.

Despite the statistics showing a rapid increase in meat consumption in Japan and Korea during the past five decades, it is important to note that Koreans and Japanese have very different traditions relating to the way in which they consume meat. Since premodern times, Japanese have deemed the handling of carcasses—both animal and human—as a source of deadly pollution. Abattoir work and leather tanning were occupations reserved for the *eta* and *hinin,* outcaste groups whose names can be translated respectively as "insurmountable filth and pollution" and "nonhuman." Although the caste/status system was formally abolished under the new code laid down by the Meiji administration during the late nineteenth century, centuries-old practices of caste segregation and discrimination persisted. Accordingly, meat did not ascend to the higher ranks of the traditional culinary hierarchy. Right up until modern times, generally speaking, Japanese continued to associate butchers with impurity and filth because of their frequent handling of animal body parts, blood, and carcasses.

During the Japanese colonial rule of Korea (1910–1945), Korean colonial immigrants to Japan tended to find themselves settling in areas adjacent to *buraku,* hamlets where the outcaste people lived, most likely due to the peripheral nature of the unmarked land on which the *buraku* people had settled. During the prewar years, conventional Japanese thinking lumped Koreans and *buraku* people together as a body of polluted, dangerous, and unclassifiable people, with their identities conflated insofar as the borderline existence of both groups was concerned. A Japanese friend recently confessed to me during a casual conversation that his family believed that a nearby butcher was of Korean origin. This is an interesting misunderstanding. For, whereas there is little statistical indication that butchers in Japan tend to be Korean, it captures the difference in meat consumption between Japanese and Koreans.

Koreans do consume meat differently from, say, non-outcaste Japanese, in that they eat pretty much every part of cows and pigs—including tongues, tripe, and organs, as well as tails in the case of cows, and feet and heads, including ears, in the case of pigs. Traditionally speaking, when Japanese killed a cow for food, they tended to remove and discard the organs; when they killed a pig, they tended to do the same, removing the organs, feet, ears, and head, discarded parts being expected to be consumed by outcastes. And, certainly, Japanese are not known for eating dog meat, whereas Koreans are. As mentioned in my Introduction, the adoption of Buddhism as the state religion during the Goryeo dynasty (918–1392) of Korea led to the prohibition of the killing of animals, but the later Mongol occupation of Goryeo led to Koreans being influenced by a Mongol diet that included a diverse range of meat products, including beef, boar, horse, lamb, pork, chicken, and duck, as well as dairy products. Prior to their contact with the Mongols, however, Koreans had always eaten dog meat. Archaeological findings show that dog meat was being consumed as early as the Three Kingdoms period (from the first to the seventh centuries) (Ouk-da Yang 2006).

Human consumption of dog meat has been recorded since ancient times (Schwabe 1979: 168). While dog meat was also eaten in prehistoric Europe, at some point in history, Europeans stopped eating it, eventually leading to dog meat consumption in Korea and elsewhere becoming the object of criticism and controversy in the eyes of contemporary Europeans and Americans. During the 1988 Seoul Olympics, the Korean government had

A *kimchi* counter at a department store in Seoul. Photo by the author.

Braving chilly mid-December weather, people wait their turn to purchase dumplings from a popular vendor in Insadong, Seoul. Photo by the author.

Naengmyeon at a food court in Koreatown, Los Angeles. A sumptuous volume of dark noodles is served, and the addition of crushed ice to the soup enhances its cooling effect. Photo by the author.

Naengmyeon at a food court in Seoul. One can see that white noodles are preferred and that more attention is paid to presentation than in Los Angeles, while portions are smaller. Photo by the author.

Jeon sold at a market in Seoul. Oversized pancakes are placed in shallow plastic colanders so that the undersides will not become soggy. Photo by the author.

Haemul pajeon (seafood and leek pancakes) at a restaurant in Seoul. Photo by the author.

A barbecued pork wrap meal *(bossam jeongsik)* served at a restaurant in Seoul. At this relatively upscale restaurant, the main dish is accompanied by many side dishes. Photo by the author.

An assortment of Japanese deli items with a Hawaiian twist sourced from a Japanese-owned supermarket. The container on the far left has seaweed salad and the one on its right chopped squid salad. Photo by the author.

Waiting line outside a Waikiki Korean restaurant. Photo by the author.

Delicious *galbi* served at a Vietnamese restaurant in Kona. Photo by the author.

Bibimbap at the Seoul Kitchen restaurant in Old Capitol Mall, Iowa City. This is the hotpot version. Photo by the author.

Jeonju bibimbap served at a restaurant in Seoul. Photo by the author.

to request that butchers remove dog carcasses from their display windows in order "not to offend American and European sensibilities" (Derr 1997: 26). Korea's dog meat consumption again became a point of contention when it came time for Korea and Japan to jointly host the soccer World Cup in 2002; the traditional method of killing dogs involved torture, as it was understood that this improved the quality of the meat ("S Korea" 2001; "Fifa Warns" 2001). Whether or not torture was involved, it was certainly true that Korean regulations associated with the production and sale of dog meat were not standardized. For example, it was only in 2008 that the City of Seoul introduced safety regulations for dog meat restaurants. At any rate, historically, Koreans have eaten dog meat and continue to do so today.

Pork was a favorite on Jeju, the island located off the southwestern coast of Korea on which my father was born and that is the home of his family lineage. There, pigs were kept under raised outhouses—a genius of recycling. Traditionally, the people of Jeju ate almost every part of their pigs, including the ears and feet. One delicacy of the island is uncooked pig's fetus pickled in spicy sauce and mixed with garlic, chili peppers, and other strong herbs. Even among Jeju natives, however, this dish would be seen as somewhat extreme, and it would be recommended that it not be consumed close to the date of an ancestral memorial ceremony for fear of polluting the sacred nature of the ritual. Pork soup was the one meal that my father cooked while I was growing up in Japan—at other times, he would not even set foot in the kitchen. Probably due to their familiarity with this animal, many Koreans from Jeju who migrated to Japan during the colonial period raised pigs, both as a source of income and a means of securing food for their families.

Raising chickens was another way of providing food commonly encountered among Korean colonial immigrants to Japan, who predominantly lived in urban areas, with women typically being involved in this activity. Many first-generation women were unable to read or write either Japanese or Korean, and it was therefore inconceivable for them to sell their chickens at markets in Japan. Home-raised chicken was a very important source of nutrition, however, for many Korean families in Japan, both during and for a long time after the colonial period. My maternal grandmother, an illiterate first-generation colonial immigrant from a southeastern province of Korea, was extremely talented at raising chickens. At the age of fifteen she was married to my grandfather, a learned man from a poor family. This match was made because my grandmother came from a low-status yet relatively well-to-do family and was thus able to bring a dowry with her. The couple migrated to Japan before they turned twenty in search of work for my grandfather. By the time my mother, the third of ten children, married my father, my grandfather owned a medium-sized factory with a dozen employees, and the family was living on a large estate that included several separate buildings near the city of Nagoya in central Japan.

Despite my grandfather's commercial success, however, my grandmother continued to live and work like a household slave, spending all of each day cleaning the entire estate, doing laundry, and cooking. In fact, she prepared three meals a day, not only for her husband and children, but also for the unmarried factory workers recruited from various parts of Japan who lived in a separate wing of the estate. Still, she continued to raise chickens. She was so good at it that her Korean neighbors would occasionally entrust her with their eggs and ask her to look after them until they hatched. When there was a family banquet, my grandmother would select a fattened chicken from among her flock of five or six. As my grandfather, an educated business owner, refused to have anything to do with the filthy task of killing chickens, my grandmother did everything—cutting the throat of the chicken, boiling it to separate the feathers, and all of the other necessary tasks. She would order us grandchildren out of the courtyard while she took care of the chicken. As a little girl, I used to imagine my grandmother performing this ritual in her native tongue; her strong provincial accent often made her Korean unintelligible to me. In my mind, her ability to kill chickens and transform them into delicious dishes was inextricably connected with her being a first-generation Korean woman whose strength often manifested itself in strange and unexpected ways.

In fact, there was little that was particularly Korean about the relationship between my grandmother and her chickens other than the fact that the raising of chickens was one of the many creative activities undertaken by colonial immigrants, especially the women, in order to put food on their families' tables. Indeed, my grandmother continued to raise chickens long after the family's financial situation had stabilized. I used to imagine that this was her way of asserting herself in a large household in which she was basically regarded as one of her husband's possessions as well as a source of labor for him. My grandfather, uncles, and aunts would unanimously comment that her chicken was far tastier and much more tender than that bought from the butcher. They would eat not only the meat but the cartilage as well whenever possible, leaving only the bare bones.

My grandmother continued raising chickens until the day my grandfather beat her so badly that he broke her rib cage as punishment for her protesting about his trip to a spa with a younger woman. After that, never again did anyone taste my grandmother's chicken. It was her way of saying: "I've had it"—using a food item in an effective manner in response to her domestic oppression.

In addition to pork and chicken, there was a distinctly colonial twist to the way in which beef was consumed by Koreans in Japan. Writing about female Korean workers at textile factories in Kishiwada, near Osaka, during the colonial period, historian Kim Chan-jeong makes an extremely interesting observation regarding tripe, now a popular item on barbecue menus in Japan. A specialist in the history of Koreans in Japan, Kim argues that the Japanese term *horumon* (tripe) is derived from *hōru mon*, an expression in the local Osaka dialect meaning "things to be discarded." This usage is closely related to the practice in which female Korean factory workers in the Kishiwada textile industry during the 1930s collected discarded tripe from butchers, marinating it in spicy sauce before grilling it and eating it outdoors (Chan-jeong Kim 1982). Now known as *horumon yaki* or tripe barbecue, this item can be found on the menus of *yakiniku* (barbecued meat, *yaki* meaning to burn or to grill and *niku* meaning meat) restaurants in Japan along with other animal parts that it was unusual for Japanese to eat, such as *motsu* (intestines), *senmai* (stomach), and *tan* (tongue).

Here, it is important to note that the terms *yakiniku* restaurant and Korean restaurant have been synonymous in Japan until quite recently. It is hard to pin down exactly how this situation came about, but it is certainly true that, historically, running a *yakiniku* restaurant was one of the very limited number of viable business options available to Korean families in Japan. *Yakiniku* eateries existed inside the Korean ghettos before the end of World War II. During the Allied Occupation of Japan (1947–1952), a period when Koreans were emerging from these ghettos to demand more rights and more humane treatment, some Korean families succeeded in setting up restaurants in more upscale, Japanese-dominated parts of urban areas. For example, a Korean woman opened a restaurant called Myeong-wolgwan (Bright Moon House) in Shinjuku in the western part of Tokyo during the late 1940s or early 1950s, which venue became a regular meeting place for expatriate Korean nationalist activists. During my first period of fieldwork spent among Koreans in Japan in the years 1992–1993, a dozen or so people assured me that this restaurant had been the launching pad for the movement representing pro-North Korean sentiment among Koreans in Japan, the majority of whom originated from the southern part of the Korean Peninsula (see Ryang 1997). The so-called ethnic food that was served at Myeongwolgwan played a more than merely utilitarian role in the development of a sense of political unity among the Koreans who gathered there to launch their new expatriate movement.

Is *Yakiniku* Korean?

In the above discussion I used the phrase "so-called ethnic food" on purpose, as it would be difficult to think of *yakiniku* as an example of traditional or authentic Korean food—it was, in fact, an invention by Korean colonial migrants to Japan. Typically, *yakiniku* restaurants in Japan are lacking in Korean-style interior décor. During the 1970s and 1980s, more upscale *yakiniku* restaurants advertised their use of odor-free *tare* (sauce) in order to appeal to Japanese customers, who disliked the smells of garlic and chili they associated with Korean cooking. In other words, when more successful *yakiniku* restaurants attempted at cutting into a larger Japanese market, they began with erasing the ethnic marker of *yakiniku,* i.e., the smell that invoked Koreanness. As Koreans in Japan became gentrified over the decades, *yakiniku* cuisine gradually lost its immigrant flavor, becoming incorporated into Japanese food. Besides, predominantly, the clientele for *yakiniku* restaurants remained Japanese. Recipes at the *yakiniku* restaurants in Japan that I approached did not align with those for *bulgogi* (barbecued food) that I had collected from South Korean sources, all of them lacking one ingredient—pears. Indeed, all thirty-five of the Korean recipe books in my collection mention pears as part of the marinade sauce for meat, whereas none of the Korean restaurants in Japan at which I made inquiries used this ingredient. Most of them had created their own "home recipes" and were, understandably, secretive about their contents. Nevertheless, they all answered in the negative to my question, "Do you use pears?"

Sweet thickened barbecue sauce, known as *tare* in Japanese, has become a staple in Japanese supermarkets, the ready-made version enabling anyone to become an instant *yakiniku* chef. The same goes for supermarket shelves in Korea, where one can find all kinds of marinade sauces for use in barbecuing meat. We can detect an important difference, however, if we compare the ingredients found in the *yakiniku* marinade sauce produced by the Japanese company Ebara and a Korean product, CJ Korean BBQ Original Sauce, for example. The former contains soy sauce, hydrolyzed vegetable protein, sugar, apples, fermented seasoning, apple vinegar, sesame oil, garlic, white sesame seeds, spices, salt, and caramel coloring. The latter, in contrast, contains soy sauce, sugar, high-fructose corn syrup, pear puree, onion puree, water, garlic, apple puree, rice wine, salt, seasoning, monosodium glutamate, green onion extract, black pepper powder, ginger extract, citric acid, xanthan gum, caramel, and roasted sesame seeds.

The conspicuous absence of MSG from the Ebara sauce aside, one ingredient used in the production of the CJ sauce caught my eye—pear puree. Though apples are used in the manufacture of both sauces, CJ's insistence on the inclusion of pear puree is telling. There is no easy way of ascertaining whether pears are more popular in Korea than in Japan, this fruit being common in both countries, being enjoyed not only as food but also in the context of poetry. In Japanese *haiku,* the flower of the pear tree *(nashi no hana)* constitutes a *kigo,* or opening phrase, indicating the spring season. In Korea, too, the fruit and flowers of the pear tree frequently appear in literature, poetry, and names. For example, the name of a well-known woman's university in Seoul, Ehwa, includes two characters symbolizing "pear" and "flowers," respectively.

Nevertheless, the Korean restaurants I am familiar with in Japan do not use pears in their marinade sauces, and the same goes for Japanese marinade sauces sold at supermarkets. The one difference in flavor produced by the generous use of fruit in general, and pears in particular, is a noticeable tanginess and subtle sweetness that sugar alone cannot create. By contrast, *yakiniku* (a synonym for Korean cuisine in Japan) is known only as spicy food. Customers at a *yakiniku* restaurant would find it odd to be asked how sweet the meat was, as the general expectation is that servings of food at *yakiniku* restaurants need to be spicy. As such, ingredients such as garlic and chili peppers fit into this notion but pears do not. Until recently in Japan, the term "Korean food" typically meant *kimchi* and *yakiniku,* both simply having to be hot and spicy.

It is very likely that cost is one of the reasons behind the absence of pears in the dishes served at Korean restaurants in Japan. After being used to produce a marinade, the thin pear slices would then have to be thrown away because of their contact with raw meat, an extremely wasteful course to take for impoverished colonial immigrants. Unless one had easy access to pear trees, one would have to buy the fruit from a store. During and after the colonial period, the majority of Koreans in Japan lived in urban areas and had no access to orchards or fruit farms, forcing them to pay market prices for fruit. Thus, I have to assume that when they first started to grill tripe on open flames during the colonial period, Koreans in Japan basically used chili powder, soy sauce, salt, and garlic. This served the dual purpose of defraying costs as well as dissipating the pungent smell of the tripe. Many older Korean women in Japan assured me that spices were important, as *horumon* would carry an unmistakable smell if prepared without them. This type of marinade—spicy and hot, and originating among the colonial immigrants—came to be known as *yakiniku no tare* (barbecue marinade) in Japan, with the Japanese version consequently typically lacking pears.

This pearless marinade, so to speak, is the historical product of colonial relations between Japan and Korea, immigrant ghetto food having been transformed into "Korean" food in Japan and then, with its pearless sauce, Japanized. Further, through this process, *yakiniku* in Japan has come to be claimed as an example of authentic Korean cuisine by Koreans living in Japan. Yet it is invisible as an ethnic cuisine, having been gentrified and Japanized over many decades after the end of colonial rule. The influx of Asian immigrants to Japan that began in the late 1980s led to the appearance of a diverse array of Asian restaurants—for example, Thai, Indian, Indonesian, and Burmese. Interestingly, the term *esunikku* (ethnic) was used to describe the food served at such establishments, while *yakiniku* and Korean food did not fall into this category, the ethnicity of the latter remaining invisible, another unmistakable legacy of the colonial era. This state of affairs somewhat parallels the way in which Korean food is embedded in other foods in Kona, Hawai'i.

The preconception that Korean food is simply hot and spicy has been steadily changing in Japan in recent decades. Since the late 1980s, the arrival of new Korean immigrants has led to the appearance of more, shall we say, authentic Korean restaurants on Japan's streets. Unlike old-timer Korean *yakiniku* restaurants operated by colonial immigrants and their advancement into the Japanese market as distinctly non-ethnic Korean food, new Korean restaurants operated by newly arrived Koreans from South Korea fully thrust their ethnic identity into Japan's food market. At one such establishment, one might, for example, encounter *cchajangmyeon,* a spicy noodle salad dish adapted from a Chinese noodle dish by Koreans in South Korea. Customers at such restaurants would also be able to appreciate that Korean cuisine amounts to more than simply *kimchi* and barbecued meat, encompassing a wide range of noodle dishes, varieties of salad, soups, differently prepared rice dishes, and dozens of different types of *kimchi*.

The arrival of these new Korean immigrants is not the only factor behind changes in the perception of Korean food in Japan, however. Globalization, the transformation of South Korea, and then, more recently and on a gigantic scale, China, into economic powerhouses, has led to concrete and significant changes in Japanese perceptions of Asia as a whole. It is no longer unthinkable for a bright Japanese college graduate to pay for a graduate education in Korea or China, and no longer is the smell of garlic ridiculed as *chōsenjin kusai,* or smelling like a Korean (a derogatory expression), namely, inferior, unsophisticated, and bad. There is even a very popular Korean restaurant franchise operated by a Japanese corporation. Of course, this does not by any means signify that ethnic discrimination itself has been eliminated. But it clearly indicates that Korean food brought by the post-1980s new Korean immigrants to Japan is different, unique, and indeed, ethnic, as compared to *yakiniku* offered by old-time colonial immigrants from Korea. This new Korean food is distinct from *yakiniku,* becoming visible as an ethnic cuisine. In such restaurants, it is common to find Korean-speaking servers, Korean-inspired décors, and wholesale use of the notion of authenticity in the menus of establishments in this category, in sharp contrast with the older-style *yakiniku* cooking, which never acquired the status of an *esunikku* (ethnic) food and, if anything, strove to erase its ethnic mark, for example, by promoting odorless grill.

I am not sure whether or not the Vietnamese restaurant in Kona used pears when marinating its *galbi,* as this dish was invisible as Korean food in Kona, served behind a different ethnic marker. Similarly, while *yakiniku* restaurants used to represent Korean food in Japan, Korean food as such was paradoxically invisible in Japan. All in all, the way in which Koreans consumed meat was seen as foreign, barbaric, and unhygienic, and was therefore hidden from public view. My Japanese friend's vague (and erroneous) association between butchers and Koreans was related to this notion: working as a butcher would mean having access to the most bizarre leftover parts for consumption possibly by the butcher's own family. *Horumon yaki* (which could be translated as "throw-away parts grill") was available only in this exotic and foreign space, removed from the domain of normal Japanese meat consumption. Thus, there is a parallel between the invisibility of Korean food in Kona and Korean meat consumption in Japan. On the other hand, there is an inversion between the Korean food in Kona and *yakiniku* restaurants in Japan. In Kona, what is Korean—that is, *galbi*—loses its authenticity, being served as part of different and diverse ethnic repertoires, while in Japan, *horumon yaki,* or grilled tripe, acquires authenticity, being served by Korean colonial immigrants whose traditions permitted the eating of such parts—parts that Japanese would ordinarily discard as inedible.

Yakiniku in Waikiki

The reader can now understand how ironic it was to me to see so many Korean restaurants in Waikiki with names that included the word *yakiniku,* as in Seoul Garden Yakiniku or Yakiniku Million. Some restaurants used the romanized version of this term, while others used *hiragana* (native Japanese syllabary) or *kanji* (Chinese characters used in the writing of Japanese) versions. Some signs even carried the term in Korean script. From this example, one can see that not only Japanese tourists but also Koreans and other Honolulu locals make use of the term *yakiniku* when thinking about Korean food. Its ubiquitous presence used in lieu of or as part of references to Korean cuisine functions as a powerful reminder of the evolution of authenticity. Because *yakiniku* has become synonymous with Korean food in Japan (via Koreans in Japan), Waikiki Korean restaurants have adopted it as a marketing device to catch the attention of Japanese tourists. Significantly, many of my colleagues and friends in South Korea and many students from South Korea have never heard of the term *yakiniku*. The way it emerges and submerges in Honolulu's touristic scenes tells an interesting side story of history that also concerns an inversion.

Reflecting historical connections between Japan and Hawai'i that go back to the pre-annexation days, Hawai'i has been one of the most popular overseas tourist destinations for Japanese since the beginning of the postwar era. In 1997, the annual number of Japanese tourists visiting Hawai'i reached an all-time high of 2.22 million. Numbers then began to decline, reflecting the moribund state of the Japanese economy and the effects of the natural disaster of 2011, but rose back up to a figure of 1.45 million in 2012. Data from 2011 show the average Japanese tourist spending $289 a day during their visits to Hawai'i, a figure almost double that for visitors from the U.S. mainland ($158). Hawai'i had a total of 7.84 million visitors in 2012, 60 percent (4.89 million) from the U.S. mainland and 20 percent (1.45 million) from Japan. By contrast, only 150,000 tourists from South Korea visited during that year (Akiyama 2013). Tokyo-based Japan Travel Bureau Corporation, one of the world's largest tourist agencies, frequently organizes package tours in collaboration with its Hawaiian counterparts. Its loyalty card, through which cardholders earn points from travel, shopping, eating out, theater attendance, and other activities, has a network of participating stores and restaurants all over Oahu, from Waikiki to the exquisite Turtle Bay resort to Haleiwa Beach, the surfers' favorite.

Japanese tourists in Honolulu are provided with advance recommendations about what and where to eat once they are in Hawai'i by guidebooks, online outlets, and other sources of information. For example, at Whole Foods Market in Kahala, a neighborhood not far from Waikiki, it feels as if half the clientele consists of Japanese tourists exchanging comments such as "Here, come here, I found it. This is what Mariko was telling me about," or "Just like my colleague Takahashi-san told me, it looks delicious." Understandably, it is more common to find such visitors in deli sections rather than in the fresh produce aisles, save for the more adventurous ones who are willing to try out tangelos and other native Hawaiian fruits and vegetables that they would not find in Japan. In the deli section of the Whole Foods Market noted above, one finds homemade kimchee (as it is spelled) at the salad bar and a Korean BBQ Chicken Bowl. I was surprised to find the kimchee more salty than garlicky, as I had generally found the food in Oahu to be loaded with fresh garlic and Maui onions when eating out in Honolulu. At one army cafeteria where I was allowed to eat, the garlic chicken I ordered was literally smothered in chopped fresh garlic, and the *ahi* (tuna) *poke* (raw fish salad) made abundant use of onions and garlic—both dishes were incredibly delicious. Therefore, the Whole Foods kimchee struck me not only as being less punchy but also—more important—as being inauthentic. As for the Korean BBQ Chicken Bowl, it was tasty, but not "Korean-tasty." On closer inspection, I found that its barbecue sauce contained soy sauce, salt, *mirin* (a Japanese fermented rice sauce), corn syrup, sesame oil, pepper, and apple paste, in addition to a spicy Korean sauce containing chili pepper, sugar, ginger, soybean paste, and vinegar. Conspicuously missing were garlic and pears. No wonder it felt un-Korean! Yet, the bowl clearly bore the name "Korean." It made me wonder whether this "Korean" taste had been created to cater to the Japanese palate, and the tourist palate in general for that matter.

Back in Waikiki, there is one Korean restaurant that is clearly well known among Japanese tourists. For days, whenever I walked past this place, there was a line of between eight and twenty-five people waiting to get in. While this establishment serves Korean food, it does not actually state this in any obvious way: the word "Korean" is just written in a small font on a menu board inside the restaurant, and the outside of the restaurant only features the words B.B.Q. and *yakiniku* written in Japanese *kanji,* not even romanized or English versions. Thus the customers, the majority of whom are Japanese tourists, come here to eat *yakiniku,* which in the minds of tourists from Japan would unmistakably signify Korean cuisine.

Yakiniku, what had been a makeshift colonial name for the food eaten by Korean immigrants to Japan, food that included animal parts the Japanese refused to eat, has come to acquire a certain authenticity across the Pacific Ocean as a term referring to Korean food. In Hawaiʻi, where Japanese peasants were brought as indentured plantation workers more than a century ago, yen-empowered Japanese tourists are offered a Japanized version of Korean food that they are familiar with via Japan's colonization of Korea. History indeed works in ironic ways.

Global Capitalism in Waikiki

As U.S. President Barack Obama and his family were vacationing in Honolulu, traffic was congested. In order to avoid driving, I set off on foot toward Waikiki Beach. As usual, the large number of Japanese restaurants were filled with crowds of Japanese (and possibly Chinese and Korean) tourists. Outside more than a few of these restaurants, lines had formed of customers waiting to be seated. Again, the effects of the Japanese tourism industry were visible, as these restaurants were most likely featured in Japanese guidebooks to Hawaiʻi, encouraging the somewhat incongruous practice of traveling all the way from Japan to Hawaiʻi to eat Japanese food. Perhaps I should not be too fast to make this assertion, as it may make Japanese food more Japanese—more authentic—to taste it in Hawaiʻi. Indeed, some of these guidebooks may rightly claim that the Japanese food found in Hawaiʻi is more authentic than that found in Japan, attempting to spark tourists' curiosity in relation to the historic Japanese presence on the islands, even though many of the chefs at these establishments may well be recent immigrants or not even Japanese at all. Scattered between the Japanese restaurants, U.S. and global franchise outlets such as Red Lobster showed their familiar faces, their menus written in Japanese and English. There were also many restaurants specializing in fusion or Hawaiian cuisine.

Hawai'i, indeed, has its own distinct cuisine, including dishes such as *loco moco* and *spam musubi* (see Yamashita 2013). Indeed, when one thinks about the ingenious Hawaiian ability to enjoy eating meat and meat products in fusion with dishes from other cultures (especially Asian cultures) that have reached the islands, *loco moco* and *spam musubi* rank as prime examples. A dish containing steamed Japanese-style white rice, a burger patty, fried eggs, and thick gravy, *loco moco* is a handy food item that includes most of the culinary necessities—fat, carbohydrates, salt, and protein—and fills an empty stomach while being delicious at the same time. There are many different versions of *loco moco* using steak, fish, or chicken, for example. One can buy *loco moco* for around $7 at a small, less touristy diner or local restaurant, or one can pay $20 for this dish at a Hilton Hotel restaurant filled with foreign tourists. In Morimoto Waikiki, an upscale Japanese restaurant where President Obama dined while on vacation in December 2013, the chef's version of *loco moco* was listed at $23. According to the menu, it uses *wagyū* (Japanese) beef, sunny-side up local eggs, and Japanese-style *hayashi* gravy.

Spam is another Hawaiian favorite, according to Kimberly Kohatsu, whose Hawaiian-raised father always kept some in the pantry of their Virginia home (Kohatsu 2012). Its popular dissemination can be traced back to World War II, when the military was served salty canned ham—known as "spiced ham," "special army meat," or spam—with surplus stock reaching populations in the Pacific. Absorbed into Hawai'i's cuisine, spam now appears in sushi form as *spam musubi* or in the form of *spam loco moco*. Kohatsu also notes that spam has the nickname "Hawaiian steak" and refers to the surprise shown by reporters when President Obama, a native of Hawai'i, ordered *spam musubi* in Oahu during one of his visits (Kohatsu 2012). In Waikiki, *spam musubi* can be found in most general stores, but the easiest place to find this dish—as well as a range of other multicultural and fusion items—is International Market Place.

Surrounded by what the forces of global capitalism would undoubtedly view as top-notch establishments, including a branch of Macy's department store, the Sheraton Princess Kaiulani, and the Hyatt Regency Waikiki Beach

Resort and Spa, International Market Place has a gross leasable area of 357,000 square feet, with 277,000 square feet of mall space. The market is packed with little shops selling T-shirts, travel bags, handmade jewelry, handblown glass artwork, paintings, craftwork, and candles—to mention only a few examples. These are predominantly inexpensive souvenir goods. In the middle is a food court. Here, one can see that the term "international" as used in the name of this mall involves a distinct focus on Asia, as one finds stands selling Chinese, Thai, Japanese, Korean, and other types of Asian food alongside others selling Hawaiian and fusion foods, all arranged in a seemingly random fashion, creating a carnival atmosphere similar to that found at a state fair.

When I'm there, I approach a Korean barbecue stand offering a slew of Korean carry-out meals. I purchase *galbi* and *bibimbap,* exactly the same items that I bought at a similar restaurant in Kona. The *galbi* comes with two large rib steaks, marinated in tangy spices and juices, cooked to perfection and served on top of steamed white rice. It is accompanied by four items that I have picked from the glass window display—again just like in Kona—potatoes, seaweed salad, cabbage *kimchi,* and potato noodle salad, or *japchae.* The *bibimbap* comes in a plastic bowl, a much more attractive form of presentation than a square styrofoam box. I break the fried egg on top of the *bibimbap,* mixing the ingredients together and noticing that the large fried egg has made the *bibimbap* look slightly similar to *loco moco.* As I taste both dishes, I notice one big difference from Kona: this restaurant is clearly catering to Japanese tourists with its Japanese-language signs asking customers to "place order here" and "pick up order here."

As I walk around the market, looking out for other food items, T-shirts, and mugs, all of the store workers tell me the same story—they need to sell everything before the city government closes down the market on New Year's Eve 2013. According to *Pacific Business News,* a developer had signed a new $87 million lease for International Market Place that involves the termination of all of the currently held leases. Where little stalls used to be found, a branch of Saks Fifth Avenue will rise (Shimogawa 2013a; Shimogawa 2013b; Shimogawa 2013c). One should not be surprised, as this is just too predictable a development. In fact, it is more surprising that it has not happened sooner—the common occurrence of forces of corporate capital running small trinket stores and food stalls out of business because they happen to occupy prime locations.

In Waikiki, almost everything is written in at least two languages, English and Japanese. Navigating through streets crowded with (mostly Japanese, but increasingly Chinese) tourists, with their armfuls of designer brand shopping bags, is a stressful endeavor, this sight mercilessly proving that global capital has triumphed in pushing concerns about natural and nuclear disasters, environmental devastation, and humanitarian crises in Japan and East Asia into the background. While a poor teenage worker in China makes less than a tenth of the minimum wage in the United States, her mega-rich compatriot drops a couple of thousand dollars on a pair of shoes—authentic designer shoes purchased directly from a commission-paying boutique, that is. This is the face of global capitalism. No doubt Saks Fifth Avenue has been attracted to Waikiki as a result of its confidence in Asian (and especially Chinese) economies and the prospect of a constant flow of trans-Pacific tourists. It is certainly true that Hawaiʻi—even crowded Waikiki—is a beautiful place, its birds, flowers, trees, fruits, beaches, sky, air, breezes and ever so frequent rainbows all magically enticing. One would not hesitate to describe the archipelago as a kind of paradise. And why shouldn't Japanese and Asian tourists come to visit? The irony is that tourism and the corporate money associated with this industry form part of a long historical process that originated with the arrival of these tourists' predecessors from Asia as indentured laborers and that continues to be sustained today by slave-like labor practices in less privileged parts of their own countries.

Sweet *Lilikoi*

Back in Kona, as I drive Highway 11 southbound, the air begins to get thinner. I am now at an elevation of around seven hundred feet above sea level. It is misty. Forbidding dark lava rocks rise on one side, followed by a pristine beach, while on the other side, lush forest climbs the slopes of a mountain that seems to reach up and touch the skirts of the clouds above. I frequently notice places where Kona coffee is grown and/or served. When they had worked out their indentured work contracts, many of the early Japanese plantation workers started up small family farms, with coffee growing being one of the more popular options. In 1914, Japanese producers accounted for more than 80 percent of the Hawaiian coffee crop, grown on more than 3,780 acres of land in the Kona district. By 1931, there were 1,300 Japanese families engaged in the growing of coffee. Early Japanese immigrants to Hawai'i have recalled that, despite their chronic poverty and debt, families were able to work together as one unit, in a cooperative fashion, and enjoying relative autonomy compared to the days they had spent working on plantations (Kimura 1988: 106–107).

Rounding a corner in the winding road, I come across a cute, picture-perfect fruit shop with a little café at the back. Having already driven for a few hours, I decide that I could use a good cup of Kona coffee. A good-looking young Caucasian woman greets me. I buy a few items—tangelos, papayas, pineapples, and a small loaf of *lilikoi* bread. The *lilikoi (Passiflora edulis)*, more commonly known as passion fruit, is Hawaiian in origin. The Hawaiian passion fruit—the yellow-looking *maracuya,* with its thick, smooth skin—differs from the wrinkly, purple-skinned-variety peel found on the U.S. mainland and elsewhere. Already impressed by the clean, well-organized interior of the store, I strike up a conversation with the owner. She tells me that the bread is her own creation, adding that she moved here from the East Coast of the United States less than ten years earlier. I thank her for making her café and parking accessible to wheelchairs, despite the fact that the lot is quite small and built along a ridge. I tell her that I tend to notice the existence of such features as my daughter has a severe disability and uses a wheelchair. The woman pleasantly accepts my compliment. In response to my question, she tells me that she gets lots of Japanese and Chinese tourists, but not so many Koreans. Back on the road, I nibble at her *lilikoi* bread; and its superb taste and moist texture cause me instantly to regret not having bought two loaves. Back at my hotel, I notice a young Korean man with his parents, whom I guess must be in their sixties. I smile to myself, impressed at the filial piety shown by this young man, who has thoughtfully brought his parents with him on a Hawaiian vacation. They are talking very softly in Korean. I feel tempted to let them know about the fruit stand and café I visited earlier that day, adding a recommendation to try the owner's wonderful *lilikoi* bread.

The fruit shop owner had made a truly long-distance move, traveling almost halfway round the globe from the East Coast of the United States to Hawai'i. The journey made by Elaine Kim's grandmother from Korea to Hawai'i was a shorter one in physical distance, and that of my grandmother from Korea to Japan even shorter still. But, I would imagine that both women experienced enormous challenges upon the completion of their respective journeys, having to deal with unfamiliar languages, cultures, and, above all, food. The changes in their daily lives must have shaken them both to their very cores, preventing them from ever changing back into the women they had once been. According to Kim, her grandmother later returned to Korea, where she spent the remainder of her days (Elaine Kim 1996: 356). My grandmother survived my grandfather, who died at a relatively young age, by four decades, dying alone in that big house near Nagoya. As I stood pondering the lives of these two grandmothers, the gentle breeze of the Kona coast cooling my face, a neat idea occurred to me: Why not marinate beef with *lilikoi? Galbi* marinated in *lilikoi,* I thought, would truly be a fusion of two Korean migrations—one precolonial and another colonial—from their homeland to places filled with so many unknowns.

4 | A Taste of Diversity

The *Bibimbap* Rice Bowl

Are There Asians in Iowa?

By the time Hawai'i fell at the hands of U.S. annexationists in 1898, Iowa had already been a U.S. state for close to half a century. According to the official version of the state's history, Iowa was "discovered" by French explorers in the 1670s. But, of course, native peoples had been living here for centuries before that, with approximately seventeen tribes living in the area now known as the heartland of America, including the Ioway, Sauk, Mesquaki, Sioux, Potawatomi, Oto, and Missouri (Schwieder n.d.). While life on the prairies was undoubtedly tough for the early settlers, increases in agricultural output led to an improvement in conditions from the nineteenth century on.

Iowa has not, however, defined itself simply as a farming state, the nation's granary, but has placed a strong emphasis on public education from early times. The 1850s saw the founding of both the University of Iowa and Iowa State College of Science and Technology (today's Iowa State University), with the respective aims of providing classical and vocational (including agricultural) education to the state's young men and women. In 1876, Iowa State Teachers' College (today's Northern Iowa University) was established with the goal of providing Iowa's public schools with well-educated and well-trained teachers. Together, these three institutions stand at the pinnacle of the state higher education sector. Aside from the high value it attaches to education, Iowa also has a great tradition of religious tolerance. Even today, diverse religious communities can be found all over the state, although each may no longer be as self-contained as it once was.

During the late twentieth century, Iowa underwent many changes, some of them fundamental. Before the industrialization of farming in the 1970s, Iowa farmers had a diverse range of livestock, often seen grazing in different parts of family-owned farms spread out over the state's rolling hills, and produced a wide variety of crops. Today, most farms are predominantly involved in the harvesting of corn, based on genetically modified seeds provided through the quasi-monopolistic Monsanto corporation, and the raising of hogs, the animals compartmentalized indoors in confined animal feeding operations (CAFOs), being kept alive only for the purpose of being fattened up and slaughtered (Joseph L. Anderson 2009; Engdahl 2007; Robin 2008). CAFOs account for more than 40 percent of world meat production today (Albritton 2009: 102). Industrialization has also had an immense financial impact on farmers. Rapid increases in production costs, the effects of property price bubbles, and further costs associated with labor and the installation of new machinery have led to an exponential increase in debt, with many family-owned farms ending up being repossessed by banks. By the mid-1980s, Iowa was witnessing the arrival of what Osha Gray Davidson has called "America's rural ghetto" (Davidson 1996). The irony is that this happened against a backdrop of ever-increasing agricultural productivity, which actually doubled between 1947 and 1979 (Albritton 2009: 58). This has only meant that, side by side with the disappearance of family farms, agriculture has become firmly placed in the monopolizing hands of a few large corporations. Thus, behind the seemingly unchanging landscape of rolling hills and cornfields much has changed in Iowa in recent years, these changes often involving cruelty to both humans and animals.

Changes have also taken place in the demographics of Iowa. As the Vietnam War drew to a close in 1975, under Governor Robert Ray (in office from 1969 to 1983), Iowa became the first state to welcome thousands of refugees from Southeast Asia, including Tai Dam, Lao, Khmer, and Hmong. Today, the state is home to a total of 52,597 persons who can trace their heritage to the Asia-Pacific region, including Thai, Japanese, Vietnamese, Laotians, Tai Dam, Filipinos, Asian Indians, Koreans, Chinese, Taiwanese, Khmer, and Burmese. While accounting for only 1.7 percent of the entire state population of a little over three million, the predominant majority of whom are white Americans, the Asian population saw a 41.3 percent increase in number between 2000 and 2012 (State Data Center of Iowa and the Office of Asian and Pacific Islander Affairs 2011).

Despite this development, Iowa continues to be characterized by white domination and racial near-homogeneity, which is a reality; but this reality also comes with a certain frame of mind, namely, denial of others' existence in Iowa. For example, take a look at reactions to a 2010 *Chronicle of Higher Education* article referring to the possible closure of fourteen PhD programs at the University of Iowa, one of which was listed as a "PhD in Asian Civilizations" (June 2010). Posts left on the *Chronicle* Web site in response to this development included one by Mark900, who wrote: "Asian civilizations? Are there any Asians in Iowa?" Countering the implication included in these questions, acostaa wrote : " . . . the very question [Mark900] poses ("Are there any Asians in Iowa?") leaves no doubt of the self-imposed ignorance and cultural insensitivity . . . "; then tomwistar jumped in, writing: "You're right, Mark900—there are no Asians in the state of Iowa. . . . Smart comments, buddy." In themselves, a few uninformed comments posted on the *Chronicle* Web site may not say much, except that it would be difficult to find many who would disagree with the assertion that Iowa is indeed a white-dominated state—whatever that may mean—both demographically and culturally.

With the above discussion as background, this chapter looks at the academic capital of the state, Iowa City, home of the University of Iowa. Here, in stark contrast to the rest of the state, an energetic process of internationalization (to borrow the current higher education jargon) is taking place in a wide variety of areas of student life, including those related to eating and finding good food to eat. Recent years have seen a rapid increase in the number of international students among its robust undergraduate population, with annual enrollment regularly surpassing the 4,500 mark. International student enrollments increased from 2,825 in 2010 to 3,271 in 2011, this latter figure representing 10.6 percent of total new undergraduate enrollments that year (Office of the Registrar, University of Iowa 2011). Of the 3,271 international students enrolling in 2011, 1,737 were from China (People's Republic of China), 383 from Korea, and 316 from India (Undergraduate Admissions, University of Iowa 2011). It is striking to look at the figures for arrivals from Korea and China and compare them with the relative size of the populations of these two countries. Proportionately speaking, there are about 6.5 times more Korean undergraduate students than Chinese undergraduate students at the University of Iowa campus, as the population of China is twenty-seven times larger than that of Korea—1,340 million and 49 million respectively in 2010. There was a further increase in numbers in the fall of 2012: of a total of 3,569 degree-seeking international students, 2,062 came from China and 416 from Korea (Undergraduate Admissions, University of Iowa 2012). In fall 2010, undergraduate tuition fees per semester at the College of Liberal Arts and Sciences were $3,882 for resident students (from Iowa) and $12,549 for nonresident students (from outside the state, including international students), with annual fees for international students therefore amounting to $25,000 (Office of the Registrar, University of Iowa 2012).

Most international students are housed in student resident halls, with meals included in the fees and menus based on what might be called standard American college fare. But, students do seek out their own places to eat outside and also occasionally cook so-called ethnic food or the kinds of food that they would eat in their home countries. Needless to say, this does not necessarily mean that they will be eating something very different: for example, McDonald's outlets are frequently found in Korea, where Western-style food is generally more popular among young people. Observed in this light, the university's international students' encounters with Korean food in Iowa City present interesting yet unexpectedly paradoxical insights into the globalization of Korean food.

Lunch-Hour Frenzy

Old Capitol Town Centre in Iowa City used to be a major downtown shopping area. After the opening of the 1,187,000 square-foot Coral Ridge Mall in 1998, complete with its ten-screen movie theater complex, NHL regulation-sized ice rink, and one thousand-seat-capacity food court, business continued to decline until the University of Iowa, located just across the street, took over the space to house its International Programs, College of Public Health offices, School of Music recital halls, walk-in clinic, IT Services, bookstores, and a number of other offices. While most of the university's offices occupy the upper level, the main level houses International Programs, a one-stop shop for international students arriving in Iowa and students who are exploring options for studying abroad. Aside from housing offices such as the Office for Study Abroad and the Office for International Scholar and Student Services, International Programs is also home to various academic centers and programs, including the Center for Asian and Pacific Studies, one of the missions of which involves hosting and sponsoring visiting scholars from East Asia and encouraging faculty collaboration with researchers in Asia.

The majority of the floor space on the main level is occupied by more than thirty retail stores and restaurants, including the university bookstore and its computer/tech store, a pharmacy, a tanning salon, a boutique, a jeweler, a bank, a vitamin store, an optician, a games store, an art supply store, a confectionery store, and a total of twelve restaurants. The foyer and hallways are filled with seats and tables with the capacity to seat about three hundred persons. Though the restaurants in this mall are small in size, people buy food and bring it into the common seating area, enabling the restaurants to serve a larger number of customers than those who can be accommodated at the tables inside their leased spaces. One of the characteristics of this mall is that its restaurants offer a diverse selection of so-called ethnic food, including sushi, fusion Indian, Chinese, Mexican, and Korean. With the addition of a new bubble tea shop in 2013, Asian-owned and usually filled with Asian customers, the mall, one may assert, is one of the most (if not the most) ethnically diverse places in Iowa City.

Let us call the mall's Korean restaurant Seoul Kitchen. Although there are only thirty-two seats inside the restaurant spread over eight closely placed tables, it serves anywhere between 100 to 120 people during its two-and-a-half-hour lunchtime. Opened only a few years ago, it has quickly gained popularity. On any given day, it is common to see about a dozen people already waiting in line outside the restaurant at around 11 a.m., despite the fact that it does not officially open until thirty minutes later. By 11:30, there is often a line of about thirty people. The restaurant had to install a picket line to clearly mark where to stand while waiting so the line would not obstruct shoppers and students passing across the mall. After the restaurant opens its doors, and as seats continue to be taken, the line continues to grow. This is not a full-service restaurant: guests have to go up to the counter to place their orders, receiving an electronic beeper and returning to the counter to collect their food when the beeper sounds. It is up to the guest to decide whether to sit inside the restaurant or in one of the seating areas outside, but the seats inside fill up quickly, making it rare to find a seat if one comes after 11:30 a.m.

The restaurant continues operating at full speed until its closing at 2 p.m. It is only open for lunch between Monday and Friday. According to a rough estimation, it serves an average of between six and seven hundred people each week. The restaurant takes a two-week break in winter and another, longer break in summer. It was closed from the end of 2011 until mid-March 2012. We were later informed that this extended closing was related to the owner's health. But as soon as it reopened after the university's spring break in March 2012, the long line of customers was back, day after day. Previously, the restaurant had opened for dinner as well, offering full-service meals from 4:30 p.m. Dinners there were much quieter—perhaps due to the fact that it was not licensed to serve alcohol and prices were about 40 to 50 percent higher than they were for lunch. A little while later, the restaurant completely stopped opening for dinner, yet the pace and intensity of its lunchtime operations went far beyond those of other comparable lunch-hour restaurants. Its menu features the regular items that one would find in any Korean restaurant in the United States, including *bibimbap* (a rice bowl with mixed vegetables), *dolsot bibimbap* (a rice bowl with mixed vegetables, served in a hotpot), *japchae* (potato noodles with meat and vegetables), *bulgogi* (barbecued beef), *galbi* (barbecued short ribs), *ojingeo bokkeum* (sautéed squid), *kimchi cchige* (*kimchi* hotpot), and *bokkeumbap* (Korean-style fried rice). Prices for lunch range from $10 to $12, making it not the cheapest option for student eating. For example, dishes at this Korean restaurant would cost $3 to $5 more than comparable ones served at a Chinese restaurant in the same mall.

So who is eating at Seoul Kitchen? While it is difficult to conduct a precise survey, my informants have told me that they believe at least two-thirds of the customers there at any given time are international students from China studying at the university. My observations during the last couple of years have confirmed this estimation. Many Korean students eat there as well, of course, but they are overwhelmed in numbers by Chinese students. On a more interesting note, my Korean informants have told me that they need to plan carefully when they intend to eat Korean food for lunch, as they become self-conscious about their breath when attending afternoon classes after eating Korean food that is made with lots of garlic and chili. Female Korean students have also told me that they tended to make do with less aromatic food, such as ham and cheese sandwiches and coffee or pizza and soda for lunch on days when they had afternoon classes. Korean female students also added that they would often take packed lunches—mostly sandwiches—when possible, as this was also more economical. I found a much greater level of this concern about the smell of particular foods among Korean female students than their male counterparts. Accordingly, it was common to see a table in the general seating area occupied by a mixed-gender group of Korean students, the females eating sandwiches or other kinds of packed lunches they had prepared at home and the males eating a hot meal from Seoul Kitchen. This may well also reflect the fact that male students are less likely to pack lunches for themselves.

Many Chinese students told me that they would alternate between the Korean restaurant and the Chinese restaurant in the mall. Most Chinese students I talked to had tried some form of Korean food back in China, but they assured me that they were eating more Korean food in Iowa City than they had done back in their home country, also remarking how much they appreciated it. In other words, they had traveled halfway around the globe only to discover the cuisine of a neighboring country. Adding another layer to this scene, a local Korean church recently started offering a free lunch once a week in the general seating area of the mall. Although the portions are not as large, this service is quite popular with international students from Korea and Korean American students affiliated with the church. Despite the arrival of this potential competitor, there has been no letup in the intensity of customer turnover at Seoul Kitchen. Given that the number of international students from China is roughly five times larger than that of students from Korea, the once-a-week free lunch provided by this church has very little impact on the way this restaurant operates—that is, simply frantically.

During one of the restaurant's lunch-hour frenzies, I had *dolsot bibimbap,* a hotpot version of a rice-bowl dish with mixed vegetables in addition to meat or tofu. As far as I could tell, *bibimbap* and *dolsot bibimbap* were far and away the most popular dishes among female customers at this restaurant, whereas male customers tended to prefer the more meaty dishes, such as barbecued beef or barbequed short ribs. The *bibimbap* served at this restaurant is superb, with a sumptuous helping of vegetables, all nicely sliced and arranged, in addition to a tasteful range of side dishes that are carefully selected so as not to clash or overlap with the vegetables contained in the *bibimbap* itself (see color plates).

After waiting in line for about twenty minutes to place an order and then another ten minutes to pick up our meal, my taster and I took a table right outside the restaurant in the general seating area since, as usual, all of the tables inside the restaurant were already taken. A family of four—grandmother, father, mother, and baby—was sitting next to us eating food from the restaurant. They were speaking Chinese, although I was unable to place which particular version of the language they were using. From their facial expressions and the way they were sharing the dishes among themselves, it was clear that they were enjoying the food. Meanwhile, the baby was drinking formula from a bottle. I wondered whether they were the family of a young faculty member or a graduate student. Either way, this young mother was able to eat something nutritious for around $10 and avoid having to cook for her elders—a state of affairs that I could appreciate as if it were my own business.

Bibimbap, a Ritual Leftover

Drawing upon her remarkable ability to use clever rhetoric, Marja Vongerichten is correct in calling *bibimbap* "a dish that magically makes use of all the odds and ends in your vegetable bin" (Vongerichten 2011: 177). Particularly after a *jesa* ancestor memorial ritual (see Chapter 2), kitchen shelves and refrigerators are likely to be filled with leftovers from dishes that were offered to the ancestors. If one were to take little bits of these dishes—some bean-sprout salad, a clump of spinach salad, a little bit of sautéed royal fern, thinly sliced meat *jeon,* and some other ingredients—before adding sliced fresh cucumber or radish and a fried egg, one would have a sumptuous *bibimbap,* a dish consisting of a bowl of rice mixed with vegetables and meat. In its vegetarian version, often one sees tofu substituted for meat. Depending on whether or not one prefers a spicier flavoring, a teaspoonful of *gochujang* or hot red paste may be added. When combining, a teaspoonful of sesame seed oil helps all of the ingredients to mix better. Most of the vegetable items will have been cooked already—sautéed, boiled, or steamed, with seasoning and spices added—during preparations for the *jesa.* In itself, therefore, *bibimbap* produces a particular flavor as it is being made, as the ingredients work on each other inside the bowl.

  Bibimbap is a dish that is not as easy to prepare in a restaurant setting as it is at home. To begin with, the chef needs to figure out how to avoid duplicating the vegetable appetizers or side dishes when selecting ingredients to go on top of the *bibimbap* rice. For example, if a restaurant were to serve bean-sprout salad and spinach salad as appetizers, the chef would prefer not to duplicate these items in the *bibimbap* itself. Also, when it comes to the vegetables that go into a *bibimbap,* many restaurants craft their own, often more Americanized, versions; for example, I have eaten a *bibimbap* that contained thin slices of tomato and iceberg lettuce. But the beauty of *bibimbap* is precisely that: one can easily create one's own *bibimbap* because this dish is, essentially, an ad hoc mixture of the ingredients one happens to have on hand. The vegetables used at most of the Korean restaurants in the United States where I have eaten *bibimbap* included sautéed zucchini, radishes, bean sprouts, carrots, and cucumbers (all thinly sliced). Meat is most often spicy sautéed ground beef or sometimes, ground pork. Where used, a tofu substitute would also have been sautéed. Sometimes, one sees a spoonful of cooked shiitake mushrooms.

In Korea, a *bibimbap* would usually contain spinach, bean sprouts, cucumber, zucchini, royal fern, radishes, and shiitake mushrooms, topped with a fried egg and one's choice of a small portion of meat. One often sees the menu item *jeonju bibimbap*, as opposed to simply *bibimbap* (see color plates). *Jeonju bibimbap* is named after Jeonju, a city in Chungcheong Province located in the center of South Korea. This does not mean that *jeonju bibimbap* is special or more authentic than other types of *bibimbap*. Rather, the term *jeonju bibimbap* denotes a standard form of *bibimbap* as opposed to a version based on a particular chef's original recipe.

Some recipe books list a few more fanciful ingredients, including chopped seaweed, sliced *muk* or buckwheat jelly, pears, and salted seafood, in addition to *doraji*, or picotee roots (Japanese morning-glory roots) that are slightly boiled, thinly sliced, and seasoned with chili-bean paste. Many books suggest that egg yolks and whites should be cooked separately in order to accentuate the contrast in their colors (Choi et al. 2007: 58–59; Kim, Han, and Kim 2005: 60–61). In the royal palace, *bibimbap* was called *goldongban,* meaning a rice dish mixed with a diverse range of ingredients, or more bluntly, odds and ends of ingredients. A royal recipe for *goldongban* by Han Bok-ryeo, a highly esteemed holder of a title recognizing her skill in the field of the royal culinary arts in Korea, includes beef as well as fish, shiitake mushrooms, *doraji*, royal fern, bean sprouts, and egg. Insofar as the ingredients are concerned, *goldongban* is not so different from *bibimbap*, but Han pays special attention to rice, insisting that it be premixed with sesame seed oil and a pinch of salt. This is because it was not regular practice at the king's table to mix ingredients in a bowl. Thus, the king would have to eat *goldongban* without mixing its ingredients, thereby requiring the rice to be pre-lubricated with oil in order to make it easier to scoop out each spoonful along with other ingredients (Bok-ryeo Han 2004: 170). Royal or not, *bibimbap* is an effective way of eating nutritious vegetables all at once, letting all of the flavors and textures create their own drama inside one's mouth.

By now, the reader will have understood why *bibimbap* is the food chosen as the theme of this chapter. A seemingly accidental mix of various ingredients meeting in a bowl of *bibimbap,* sometimes requiring an extra lubricant such as sesame seed oil and sometimes needing a kick to be added to the taste through the use of red chili paste, is a perfect metaphor for the diversity and internationalization that is happening currently on the University of Iowa campus. In fact, this has become a common scene on higher education campuses across the United States. Diverse ingredients should mix to create a unique, improved flavor, a flavor that each ingredient on its own would not have, and a flavor that is superior precisely because it is produced by different peoples commingling and working together. True—each of the ingredients comes to the bowl from a different source. Some are surplus items from a *jesa* ceremony held a week earlier; others are small amounts of leftovers from the previous day's lunch or dinner; while yet others have been freshly bought from a store. Mixed together, they all play meaningful roles in the constitution of this dish. To return to the university analogy, some students discovered the University of Iowa due to intensive international recruitment efforts on the part of the admissions office; others came here from coastal U.S. cities; and yet others are here because their parents and grandparents attended this university. Mixed together, ideally they should create a seemingly better entity than each of them could have done alone. Is this working, though, I wonder?

Food in Iowa

There are other aspects of Iowa that international students from Korea or China would most likely miss while studying at the University of Iowa. Iowa is one of the main providers of food to the rest of the United States and over 90 percent of its 55,875 square miles of land is used for farming. Iowa is one of the top-ranking states in both corn and soybean production, harvesting 2.37 billion bushels of corn ($9.47 billion in value) and 439 million bushels of soybeans ($4.78 billion) in 2007. It is ranked second nationally in red meat production, with 6.6 billion pounds produced in 2007. It also leads the nation in hog, egg, cheese, milk, turkey, and wool production. In 2007, Iowa ranked second in the nation in terms of total agricultural exports and third in terms of farm cash receipts ("A Look at Iowa Agriculture" 2010). The largest manufacturing sector in Iowa is the food-processing industry, which includes meatpacking (canned ham, sausages, etc.), cornstarch and corn sugar production, and cereal and popcorn processing.

As mentioned at the beginning of this chapter, farming in Iowa has departed significantly from its earlier focus on a diverse range of crops. Iowa farmers are increasingly placed under the control not simply of U.S. capital, but global, multinational capital. National governments, especially those in OECD countries, often condone or act in sync with the activities of global capital, resulting in long-term damage to human health and the environment, and Iowa is no exception. Powerful farm chemicals (from DDT to Round-up) have caused much irreparable and irreversible damage to Iowa's soil, wetlands, and water. The problems now faced in Iowa are not isolated ones—indeed, they are part of today's globalizing world. While biotechnology and industrial farming dominate the West and destroy farmland, it is rare in other parts of the world, such as most parts of Africa, where crops are more commonly destroyed by insect infestations and drought, resulting in food shortages (Paarlberg 2009).

Yet, the truth about food production is far from readily available. Anyone who has watched the film *Food, Inc.,* directed by Robert Kenner, will see that many processed industrial food items are now produced in a genuinely mechanical manner at a variety of sites. These range from densely packed cattle ranches to overcrowded windowless henhouses in which chickens are overfed in artificially short periods of time and stuffed with antibiotics and growth hormones. Meanwhile, a control system is used in the production of ground beef in the U.S. Midwest that oversees ammonia levels at multiple locations around the nation. Through the appearance of such uncanny scenes, farmers lose their autonomy and independence, while the food that we buy from our local supermarket starts to look alien (Kenner 2009).

As an agricultural state, Iowa is located front and center of such developments. There may be hardly any shortage of food, but anxiety gravitates toward issues of food safety and quality, given an intense level of corn dependency in most of processed food production on one hand and the rising monopoly of genetically modified corn seeds by a handful of corporations such as Monsanto on the other. While Iowa strives to introduce wind energy and adopt other sustainable approaches to farming, it finds itself caught between the pros and cons of ethanol production, which uses corn. Due to successful lobbying by major oil, seed, and corn (for ethanol) producer

Archer Daniels Midland Company (ADM), the crop price has increased since 2006, basically resulting in a multiplication of profits for ADM while denying small to mid-scale farmers access to any benefits (Hauter 2012: 37, 65). Today, corporate farming and fossil fuel production have become so indissolubly connected that they are now locked into one solid chain of production and distribution connecting ConAgra to Shell Oil to Walmart. As Robert Albritton writes: "Indeed, as time has passed our food has become more and more petroleum-intense, as it has taken more and more calories of petroleum to produce one calorie of food. By the beginning of the twenty-first century it took on average ten calories of fossil fuel to produce and deliver one calorie of food, excluding household storage and cooking, which also use a lot of fossil fuel" (Albritton 2009: 58). Even the method by which Iowa's crops are transported today—through a dependence on fossil fuels and over enormous distances—is unsustainable and harmful to human well-being in the long run (Mintz 2008).

Scholars have energetically studied globalization and food—including the ways in which food has traveled in time and space, both historically and contemporarily. Fascinating discoveries have been made, from the realization that cooking is a fundamentally human activity to the understanding that sharing food is even less common among animal species. Writers through the ages have related their encounters with various kinds of exotic foods, while others have succeeded in making such exotic foods their own (Bestor 2004; Bestor 2005; Civitello 2008; Freedman 2008; Goody 1998; Inglis and Gimlin 2009; Jones 2007; Lévi-Strauss 1964; Lien 2009; Nützenadel and Trentmann 2008; Tannahill 1973; Watson and Caldwell 2005). I contend, however, that what we refer to today as the globalization of food differs fundamentally from the prehistoric spread of barley, the ancient import of olives from Greece to Rome, or the transmission of spices between continents along the Silk Road. As the forces of multinational and transnational global capital have come to play a key role in determining how the foods we eat are produced, distributed, and consumed, a mutation has taken place in the nature of food transmission, resulting in the gross exploitation of humans, including both producers and consumers. It is said that the human population today is divided into three categories: the 1.2 billion overeaters, who eat 850 kilograms of grain each year; the 3.5 billion sustainers, who consume 350 kilograms of grain a year; and the 1.2 billion who are barely surviving on a mere 150 kilograms or less of grain each year (Kimbrell 2002: 9). An uneven food supply and an ever-widening gap between rich and poor are prominent and concrete results of globalization (Harvey 2005; McNally 2006).

As globalization ever so powerfully impacts Iowa's farmland, unexpectedly (or perhaps it is wholly logical), Korea emerges as an important counterpart. In fact, Korea and Iowa are closely, if indirectly, connected in the areas of food production and the import and export of food. In the previous chapter we noted the exponential increase in meat and animal product consumption in South Korea during the last few decades. In the early 2000s, South Korea was the third-largest market for U.S. beef, with an annual value of approximately $850 million ("South Korea Relaxes US Beef Ban" 2008). But Korea severely restricted imports of U.S. beef in 2003 when it was discovered that it was contaminated by so-called mad cow disease, leading to a reduction in the volume of U.S. beef imports from 246,595 tons in 2003 to a mere 672 tons in 2004 ("Total US Beef Exports" 2009). With the signing of the free-trade agreement between South Korea and the United States in 2007, the U.S. livestock sector is being directly impacted by the resumption of beef importation by South Korea. A study by researchers at the Center for Agricultural and Rural Development, Iowa State University, predicts that the U.S. share of Korea's beef import market will increase from 0.21 percent in 2006 to 36 percent in 2016 (Fabiosa, Hayes, and Dong 2007). In 2008, U.S. beef ranked second after Australian beef, accounting for 20.9 percent of all imported beef in South Korea ("US Beef Popular Again" 2008). By 2010, South Korea was back as the world's third-largest importer of U.S. beef ("S. Korea Becomes World's Third Largest" 2010). The free-trade agreement led not only to the removal of duties on beef but also on other key Iowa products such as corn and soybeans. This is a significant development, as South Korea is also the third-biggest buyer of corn (Sungwoo Park 2012). As the Iowa State University researchers note: "The terms of this agreement are unusually aggressive in that the United States has never before managed to obtain a zero tariff, zero quota agreement with a densely populated Asian country that has a significant agricultural industry" (Fabiosa, Hayes, and Dong 2007).

Of course, this would mean that South Korean livestock farmers are directly set against their U.S. counterparts, including those in Iowa. In 2008, tens of thousands of South Koreans protested against the free-trade agreement with the United States, referring to the then President Lee Myung Bak as "Lee Wan Yong," an infamous national traitor who is considered to be the person who bore the greatest responsibility for allowing Korea to be colonized by Japan in 1910 (Choe 2008). Protestors threw a bucketful of dung at a beef counter in a prestigious Lotte Mart supermarket, forcing six of its fifty-three franchised stores to stop selling beef in July 2007 (Hwang 2007). Korean beef farmers continue to worry about their current losses and their bleak future, struggling to deal with a rapid fall in the price of Korean beef cattle and made to feel that they will be unable to compete in a market saturated with imported U.S. beef ("Beef Farmers Full of Worry" 2007). More recently, upon receiving word of an outbreak of mad cow disease in California, Korean retailers briefly stopped beef imports from the United States, only to resume them immediately ("US Beef Pulled from South Korean Shelves" 2012; "South Korean Retailer Reinstates US Beef" 2012). Thus, whether intended or not, the well-being of Iowa farmers seems to be closely connected with that of Korean farmers and the Korean economy at large.

A glance at Iowa's agricultural statistics might lead us to believe that the state's farmers are earning increasingly larger incomes. While the price of corn averaged $1.94 in 2005, it was estimated to rise to $6.05 in November 2011; the price of soybeans also increased (from $5.54 to $11.40) over the same six-year period ("2011 Farmland Value Survey" 2012). But Iowa farmers are seriously concerned about a possible bubble effect in relation to their farmland. According to a land value survey carried out by Iowa State University (which has been undertaking this task for the past sixty-one years), land values increased by 32.5 percent between 2010 and 2011, which represents a doubling of the previous year's increase of 15.9 percent ("2011 Farmland Value Survey" 2012). This is similar to the situation immediately preceding the farmland bubble of the early 1980s, which led many Iowa farmers to lose their properties and declare bankruptcy.

The proportion of Iowa's total farmland owned by corporate entities and investors increased from 18 percent in 1989 to 39 percent in 2005. Closer inspection reveals that corporate control is also encroaching on the agricultural sector in more subtle ways. For example, an increasing number of independent chicken farmers are now being pushed into entering highly restrictive multiyear contracts with corporations as a result of their monopolistic control of the market. Once locked into such contracts, farmers become subject to corporate policy relating to such issues as how to raise their chickens, how much feed to use, and what amounts of hormones and antibiotics to give the birds in order to fatten them up within what the corporation considers to be an optimal period of time, often forcing farmers to take out loans in order to purchase company-designated machinery and comply with company directives relating to cost-effectiveness and efficiency in production. Even though farmers may own their own land, corporations exert an increasing degree of control over their activities through financial intervention and regulation of the means of production. Also, as a consequence of globalization, the prices of oil and energy now directly impact the price of corn, while movements in commodity prices on Wall Street have an influence on the rise and fall of local land values (all data are from "2011 Farmland Value Survey" 2012). As is the case elsewhere, globalization is making the lives of Iowa farmers more vulnerable and more easily affected by shifts in the world economy.

Memories of family farming origins continue to live on in the minds of Iowans for many generations. Many years ago, I offered a class at the University of Iowa involving a life-history project. Each student was required to interview an older member of his or her family. Predictably, many students opted to interview their grandmothers. When I read their papers, I was struck by the more or less ubiquitous emphasis on food in the lives of members of their grandmothers' generation. Recollections of Christmas dinners on the farm as a child, the first Thanksgiving turkey cooked as a new bride, or the wedding banquet given for their daughter abounded. The student papers were filled with delicious food stories. However, not all of these were happy, some recalling tough times on a farm trying to scavenge what little was left for the family to eat.

Students also told funny stories of how mixed-up ingredients eventually turned into a family recipe. Indeed, Iowa has a rich trove of farm recipes, and farming families enjoy a diverse range of meals not simply following a "meat and two vegetables" formula. Traditional as well as innovative recipes continue to be served at Living History Farms near Des Moines, where lifestyles and practices related to the cultivation, harvesting, and the preparation of food on Iowa's traditional farms are preserved, while many historic landmarks have been converted into inns and restaurants where one can encounter unexpectedly innovative menus (Anderson and Matelic 1980; Painter 2008). This, in turn, is a testimonial to how much of our past has been lost. No longer do we have a farm food, if you like, a food that is offered in a farm using its diverse crop and produce. Instead, we see familiar labels of mass-produced food cans and containers in the pantry of farm houses of Iowa.

The Other Iowa

Although one associates Northern European immigrants with farming and food production in Iowa, more recent years have seen it become the norm for immigrants from Eastern Europe, Latin and South America, and Asia, especially Southeast Asia, to enter the food-processing industry. While international students from China or Korea study at the University of Iowa, thousands of former refugees, immigrants, and their descendants from neighboring Vietnam, Laos, Cambodia, and Burma work in Iowa's meatpacking plants and other food-processing facilities. As already noted, Iowa accepted a large number of Southeast Asian refugees in the wake of the Vietnam War, and a great many of them now work in the meatpacking industry in northwestern Iowa. Though Iowa has an almost infinitesimally small Asian minority (1.7 percent of a total three million population), this population displays a disproportionately large degree of diversity and disparity on many fronts—from culture, language, and history to class background, education level, and social status. Here is another Iowa that is largely unfamiliar to the majority of Iowans, let alone to the population of international students from Asia.

Looking at this Asian population in Iowa, the first thing one notices is a pronounced degree of economic disparity. According to state-compiled data, the median income of Asian households in 2010 was $53,431, $4,849 above the Iowa average of $48,585. Yet, at 14.2 percent, the poverty rate among Asians in Iowa was 3 percent higher than the state average of 11.5 percent (Office of Asian and Pacific Islander Affairs 2010). Together, these statistics reveal that there is greater income disparity among Asians in Iowa than among members of the state population at large. Furthermore, it has been recorded that, proportionately speaking, Asians in Iowa have a higher mortality rate from cancer than white Iowans. According to 2010 statistics, cancer was the cause of death of 42.9 percent of Asians aged between forty-five and fifty-four, as opposed to a figure of 32.8 percent for white Iowans, and the cause of death of 36.8 percent of Asians between the ages of sixty-five and eighty-four, as opposed to a figure of 28.7 percent for white Iowans of the same ages (Iowa Department of Public Health 2010).

Intrigued by these statistics, I sought internal funding from the University of Iowa under the project title "At Risk in Iowa: Healthcare Disparities among Iowans of Asian Heritage." In 2008, the University of Iowa Office of the Vice President for Research granted funding for this project under the Social Sciences Research Funding program, enabling me to conduct preliminary research and leading to the production of a health-care information booklet in six different Asian languages in addition to English in collaboration with Henny Ohr, a former executive director of the state's Commission for Asian and Pacific Islanders in its Department of Human Rights. She and I conducted five focus-group meetings among members of a diverse range of Southeast Asian ethnic groups in Des Moines—Tai Dam, Vietnamese, Lao, Cambodians, and multiple ethnic groups from Burma— during the years 2010–2012. These meetings resulted in the emergence of interesting data showing the considerable level of anxiety suffered by Asians in Iowa in relation to difficulties in gaining access to quality health care and maintaining a healthy lifestyle due to cost, on one hand, and to their lack of cultural proficiency and knowledge of English, on the other. Some believed that their doctors treated them differently from how they treated their Caucasian patients. Many found the largest problem was the lack of adequate interpretation services.

Most interestingly in the context of the present study, I discovered that there was a close connection between Asians' concerns about health care and their dissatisfaction with the food items that were available locally. Older immigrants in particular expressed concern over the lack of availability of traditional food items and medicinal herbs in Iowa. To order them from specialty stores in other states where Asians had greater visibility, such as California, meant paying higher prices. A few of the older Asians in Des Moines whom I met remarked how much they longed to eat a simple meal that was authentically theirs. They often commented that no matter how rich and nutritious an American meal might be it did not satisfy them; as one put it, "It does not matter how much I eat [American food], because my stomach remains empty." According to them, it was difficult to prepare a simple dish that primarily used vegetable ingredients in Iowa. A visitor to one of the largest and most popular Asian grocery stores in Des Moines would immediately notice a difference when comparing it to its counterparts in Iowa City, which are Korean- and Chinese-owned. Here in Des Moines, Asia means Southeast Asia. Reflecting dietary differences between East Asia and Southeast Asia, the store smells different, looks different, and feels different. The shelves are lined with a huge selection of canned foods bearing labels in various Southeast Asian languages. Vietnamese bakery items look particularly enticing. But one notices a conspicuous absence of fresh produce in comparison to the East Asian/Korean supermarkets of Baltimore discussed in Chapter 2.

Unlike the international students from Asia, who typically have the means to enjoy the Asian food served at restaurants, Iowans of Asian heritage have to try to satisfy themselves and get by using whatever limited resources they possess when it comes to obtaining a diverse range of food and medicinal items. Each ethnic community places an emphasis on traditional festivals held in their own community centers, where communal cooking and the sharing of food are focal activities for participants. But once the communal festivals are over, people go back to their state of lacking the food they crave—ironically, in a society where food is abundant. After all, if you are what you eat, in the context of diaspora we need to reword this statement: you are what you do not and cannot eat.

Globalization at Home

Final exam week is near on the University of Iowa campus and the students are getting a little tense. I take a seat at a corner table to have my sandwich in the mall—I only have a little over half an hour before my next meeting at 2:30 p.m. A group of Asian students takes a table right next to me. As there are six of them, they put three tables together and move six chairs. As I glance at them, the four male and two female students are talking in Korean. I try to have a good look, wondering if I know any of them, but there is no one that I recognize. Before long, their beeper rings. I gather that they have been waiting their turn to pick up the food they ordered from Seoul Kitchen, which is right opposite where we are seated. As I look over, Seoul Kitchen is serving the last group of customers for that day before closing at 2 p.m. Soon they return, each carrying a tray of food. I see that four of them, including the two female students, are having *bibimbap,* and the other two *sundubu,* a spicy tofu hotpot. Given the strong flavor of the latter dish, I gather that the two students who have ordered it do not have afternoon classes. Paying no attention to me—and without entertaining the possibility that I might be able to understand their language—they begin talking about their studies—how difficult they find some of their classes, how much they enjoy certain others, and so on. My ears perk up as they go on to compare two local Korean groceries in Iowa City. Apparently, they all live closer to one of the markets, and though they want to go to the other one, they do not have a vehicle. They are trying to figure out what time to take the first bus to the depot in order to change lines there and catch another bus to their destination. As I wonder what the reason might be for them needing to go to the other store, which is located farther away and requires changing bus lines en route, my time is up. I hurry toward the exit on my way back to the campus.

As I am about to leave the building, I notice a group of African American teenagers gathering outside. I realize that today is Thursday, the day on which classes at Iowa City community schools finish one hour earlier than usual. As some talk loudly and joke about something using exaggerated gestures, some girls begin dancing. As I walk past the bank located immediately inside the mall, that is, close to the exit where the teenagers are gathered, two uniformed security officers emerge from the bank, their chests thrust forward and arms crossed in a conspicuously intimidating manner. The teenagers do not notice and keep on talking loudly and moving around. I have to hurry back to my building across the street. As I turn back and take one last look at the scene, the teenagers are now getting on a bus. I try to see whether or not the security men are still there. From my distant vantage point, it appears that no one is standing in front of the bank any more.

When we first moved to Iowa City from Baltimore in 2006, I noticed that some establishments in town were hypersensitive to the kind of scene I had become so accustomed to seeing in Baltimore, one that I would register as innocuous—teenagers are loud just about everywhere in the world. But, there is an unmistakably intensified security presence—in the form of private security firm employees or police officers—whenever groups of African American teenagers congregate in one place in Iowa City. This is despite the fact that African Americans, just like Asians, account for an extremely small proportion of the local population. A large portion of Iowa City's low-income African American population relocated from the Chicago area relatively recently. Based on interviews with African Americans in Iowa City, Danya Keene, Mark Padilla, and Arline Geronimus have documented the lack of acceptance of African American residents by the larger (read: white) community of Iowa City: "[The African Americans'] quest for opportunity in Iowa bring them to a whiter community where they confront head-on the systems of racial exclusion that have produced the profoundly unequal geographic distribution of resources and opportunity that they seek to escape" (Keene, Padilla, and Geronimus 2010: 282).

At the end of that day, I hurry toward my car, which is parked on the other side of the mall from the campus, thus requiring me to walk through the mall many times a day. I am on my way to pick up my daughter from an after-school-care program for persons with disabilities. I do not want to be late, but it is already what we call "rush minute" in Iowa City, meaning that there will be a very minor degree of traffic congestion, perhaps just enough to increase my traveling time by five minutes or so. I am already cutting it close in my rush to make it by the arranged pickup time. I quickly walk past a nail salon run by a Southeast Asian family. As is the case at many Southeast Asian business establishments, this one has a small electric fountain and a little statue of the Buddha, ritual objects meant to improve business prospects. I see this establishment almost every day during a week because of my parking spot. Not once, however, have I seen an Asian customer, or any customer of color, for that matter, inside; the unchanging scene is one of Asian workers polishing the fingernails and washing the feet of white customers. I wonder if the owners' children are also attending college or whether they may not have the opportunity or financial capacity to do so. Certainly, I would imagine, it would be difficult for them to send their children abroad to study, like the Korean and Chinese students at the University of Iowa who pay close to $100,000 in tuition fees over a four-year period, many spending $12 on *bibimbap* for lunch at a place like Seoul Kitchen. Thinking about this as I insert my credit card into the machine to pay for my parking ticket, I am reminded that there is a close connection between globalization and the creation and reinforcement of huge disparities between peoples and nations.

Bibimbap's Authenticity

Early on, I commented that *bibimbap* was a dish that could be created out of an ad hoc mixture of leftover dishes. The term *bibim* comes from the verb *bibida,* meaning to rub or mix together. As such, theoretically speaking, mixing any dishes with rice or *bap* in a bowl would lead to the creation of one version of *bibimbap*. We already saw in Chapter 1 that *naengmyeon* mixed with vegetables and hot bean paste is called *bibimnaengmyeon,* or mixed spicy noodle salad. This makes *bibimbap* one of the most creative dishes in Korean cuisine. But this freewheeling nature of *bibimbap* puts us in a quandary. For, if *bibimbap* can be created ad hoc, how does one determine its authenticity? After all, does authentic *bibimbap* even exist? Earlier, I mentioned that *jeonju bibimbap* often stands out as a more traditional form of *bibimbap* among versions of this dish served at restaurants in Korea. Such restaurants would not, however, have an item simply called *bibimbap* on their menus in addition to *jeonju bibimbap*. In fact, one would find either one or the other: they are interchangeable. This does not mean that all *bibimbap* are like *jeonju bibimbap*. At a Buddhist temple in Korea where I had a monk's version of *bibimbap*, I noticed the notably dull colors of the vegetables used by the kitchen there. Rather than trying to make the bowl look more festive—as is suggested in cookbooks, through the use of carrots, for example, or by cooking egg yolks and whites separately in order to accentuate the diversity of colors—the vegetables used at the temple were basically ferns, spinach, and picotee roots. Even red-bean paste was abstained from in the temple due to its vivid color, as well as its strong flavor.

Much to my fascination, I was served a nearly identical version of *bibimbap* on one of my Korean Airline (KAL) flights to Seoul in 2010, the only notable differences being the providing of a small container of red sauce and a tiny serving of ground beef. The passengers seated next to me were Koreans, and they used up most of the sauce while eating the dish. The KAL menu simply referred to it as *bibimbap,* without any further elaboration nor any reference to whether or not it was a Buddhist version of this dish. (In fact, it could not have been, due to the inclusion of a small amount of ground beef.) Yet, the KAL *bibimbap* was far removed from the conventional version of *jeonju bibimbap*, which comes with many brightly colored vegetables, with an emphasis on visual pleasure as well the use of signature spices.

Can one, after all, have authentic *bibimbap* when the very name of the dish dictates that odds and ends of vegetables be mixed together with rice in a bowl? If, by definition, authenticity demands that the qualities and elements of a dish be unchangeable and original, there cannot be any room for creativity or spontaneity—such as that involved when putting any leftover dishes one finds on a refrigerator shelf into a rice bowl and calling it *bibimbap*. Yet *bibimbap* is truly that—a dish created by an ersatz assortment of odds and ends. In the Conclusion, I shall discuss this and other questions relating to authenticity that we have encountered so far.

Conclusion

Korean Food at Multiple Sites

In his seminal essay proposing the emergence of the multisited ethnography, George Marcus wrote: "For ethnographers interested in contemporary local changes in culture and society, single-sited research can no longer be easily located in a world-system perspective. This perspective has become fragmented, indeed, 'local' at its very core . . . " (1995: 98). One of the pivots of this new ethnographic method, multisited ethnography, Marcus continued, would involve the "follow the thing" technique, which, according to him, was best exemplified in Sidney Mintz's study of the production and consumption of sugar (1985). That study, set on a global world-historical scale encompassing transatlantic colonialism, played a significant pioneering role in bringing power relations—more precisely, uneven power relations—to the center of the study of food. As an example of ethnography, however, *Sweetness and Power* (Mintz 1985) is an anomaly. To begin with, no conventional ethnographic fieldwork was involved in the production of this book, the bulk of Mintz's research having been conducted amid archives, documents, and historical studies. Yet, along with Marcus, I regard Mintz's work to be as ethnographic as any of the other so-called classical ethnographic texts might claim themselves to be. Although it includes no quotations from structured or unstructured interviews, for example, Mintz provides a clear and considered analysis of the various contingencies involved in the history of sugar, its effects on the lives of the individuals involved—whether in relation to the semi-artificially created need for white sugar or to the strange consequences of the rise of the working class in England for slavery across the Atlantic. In the foregoing pages,

I have tried to emulate Mintz, on a much smaller scale and within a limited time frame, in following some of the journeys taken by Korean food, concentrating on the United States but with detours to South Korea, North Korea, and Japan.

Marcus published his article in 1995. Almost twenty years later, despite the existence of a number of inevitable limitations, I have found his proposed concept to be an effective one in the context of the present study. My quest to follow the journeys of Korean food from Korea to the United States pushed me from one location to another, both temporally and spatially, along historic and geographic axes, across the United States, to South Korea, North Korea, and Japan, moving through Korea's colonial era to national partition after World War II, moving forward again to the post-1965 era with its influx of Korean migrants to the United States, and then to the current climate of internationalization in the U.S. higher education system. In doing so, I encountered more than one example of colonialism, more than one example of annexation, more than one example of migration, and more than one example of diaspora. While I concentrated on an examination of four food items at four different locations, the reader will have noticed that the theme of my project progressively broadened in scope, and inevitably so, due to the very nature of the process by which food circulates in a globalized world—namely, with enormous speed and intensity. Yet, as the reader will also recognize, my ethnographic examples have told us stories not only of speed but also of the lack thereof, in addition to stories not only of food that has been widely disseminated and appreciated but also of food that has been forgotten.

Stories of Food

My encounter with *naengmyeon,* or chilled chewy noodle soup, in Los Angeles, discussed in Chapter 1, was admittedly brought about by accident after I had been unable to find another restaurant where I had previously eaten spicy sautéed calamari. However, in the end, this experience turned out to be no accident. The unbleached, MSG-free LA *naengmyeon* brought back memories of the *naengmyeon* I had had in Pyongyang in North Korea decades earlier. Following this memory led me to trace the route by which *naengmyeon,* a popular food-court item in Seoul, had been introduced to South Korea through the massive influx of refugees from the northern half of the peninsula during the Korean War (1950–1953). As such, the chewy noodles used in the *naengmyeon* I had in LA's Koreatown bore in their texture the history of national partition, civil war atrocities, Cold War tension, and the multiple displacements of Koreans during the latter half of the twentieth century. Viewed against this historical backdrop, it is no longer clear whether the *naengmyeon* in Pyongyang today is more authentic than that served in Seoul or Los Angeles, or for that matter in Dandong or Abu Dhabi. Except for the consistently chewy texture of the noodles, other features of this dish, such as the color and the contents of the broth, have come to vary depending on the location. One could argue that each different version is based on an original recipe. But what does that say about any claim to authenticity? Did authentic *naengmyeon* even exist in the first place?

As we saw in Chapter 2, the metamorphosis of *jeon,* or pancakes, from a ritual food offered during ancestor memorial rites *(jesa)* to a portable and packable carry-out favorite of Korean restaurants and supermarkets in the United States, tells a story of its own—a story of a decontextualized food item the sacred meaning of which has been transformed into a commercially viable product line in the global food market. The large Korean supermarkets that I discovered in the suburbs of Baltimore, with their massive displays of *jeon* and other examples of packaged ethnic food, represent the rise of global capital. As we saw, small local corner stores have been squeezed out, despite having managed to survive for many years in tough inner-city environments prior to the arrival of ethnic corporate capital. Here, the transformation of *jeon* from ritual food to portable finger food has not been so much about its content or form as about its position or location within the context of the globalizing food market. When found out of its original context, severed from its ritual role as a vehicle for briefly paying respects to one's ancestors, *jeon* evokes a sense of disconnection, even sadness. Instead of continuing its sacred role as a form of ritual offering, *jeon* today brightens restaurant tables and supermarket shelves throughout the United States—and also in Korea. One could simply accept this as one of the effects of globalization, or more precisely, capitalist globalization, where just about everything is turned into a commodity and linked to the pursuit of profit. Indeed, in the capitalist economy, original meanings often get replaced by mass-produced or reproduced ones that exist purely to facilitate the global circulation of commodities. Does this mean that *jeon*'s authenticity has long been lost? How are we to understand this?

My discussion of meat consumption in Chapter 3 was combined with the stories of two examples of colonialism—the annexation of Hawai'i by the United States and the annexation of Korea by Japan. The reader will have noted an immense degree of complexity surrounding the parameters involved in the act of eating meat: how to prepare it, which parts of an animal to eat (or not eat), which animals to eat (or not eat), what to marinate the meat in, how to understand the meat-eating habits of others, and so on. These are not inconsequential matters, as they are directly connected to the issue of who regards whom as being less civilized and more barbaric. For example, eating animal organs or pig's feet is unacceptable to Japanese, while eating dog meat is repugnant to Europeans. Indeed, how people are labeled appears to be more dependent on what meat rather than what vegetables they eat. For example, the fact that dogs are eaten in parts of Asia but not in Europe may be related to the fact that they have been seen as work companions during the long history of livestock raising in Europe, whereas in East and Southeast Asia, where rice cultivation has traditionally been dominant, they have been viewed as somewhat redundant. Looked at in this way, dog meat consumption in Korea, an oft-cited source of European outrage, has its own legitimate historical context.

The absence of Korean restaurants and ubiquitous presence of Japanese restaurants in Kona, Hawai'i, on the one hand, and the unexpectedly delicious *galbi* barbecued beef served at a Vietnamese restaurant at the same location on the other, speak to the uneven remnants of Korean and Japanese migrations to Hawai'i and Japan's colonial rule of Korea. Similarly, the fact that the *yakiniku* barbecue is synonymous with Korean cuisine in Japan bears witness to colonial encounters between Korean immigrants to Japan and the mainstream Japanese population. In the case of *yakiniku*, a colonial recipe came to acquire identification as Korean food, which, paradoxically, remained invisible in contrast to other ethnic (*esunikku:* read Asian) foods in Japan. In Kona, Korean food was found embedded in other Asian food items (excluding Japanese ones). As such, it has lost its property of being exclusively Korean. Then, in Honolulu, we saw *yakiniku* reemerging as a signifier of Korean food, catering to Japanese tourists in Waikiki and elsewhere. These strange tales of *galbi* and *yakiniku*, one dish invisible in some parts of Hawai'i and another hypervisible in certain other parts, capture some of the ironic turns effected by colonial and postcolonial histories, with ample allusions to the possibility of further turns to come in this age of global capitalism.

Finally, in Chapter 4, we visited a small Korean eatery located adjacent to the University of Iowa that is thriving in spite of the fact that it only operates during weekday lunch hour. We noted that many of the restaurant's patrons are drawn from the cashed-up ranks of international students from China, the scene set against the background of a wave of Chinese dominance in the internationalization of the U.S. higher education market. This meeting between Chinese students and Korean food in Iowa City tells the story of globalization eloquently. Yet a different kind of internationalization or globalization also exists in Iowa—that which is found in the stories of former refugees and new immigrants. They long for the food of their homelands, the food they used to eat before coming to the United States, a land of hamburgers and fried chicken. Here, in the lives of diasporic people, the lost food of their homeland serves as a marker of their identity; that is to say, their inability to gain access to such food items is, in itself, a constitutive element of their identity. This being the case, the popularity of a Korean restaurant among international students at the University of Iowa is an illusory and transient example of globalization, although this does not mean that the phenomenon is any less significant. For the fact that hundreds of Chinese students in Iowa (and by the same token, thousands of Chinese students throughout the United States) not only can afford to pay full tuition fees as international students but also eat lunch almost every weekday at a moderately priced Korean restaurant vividly, albeit partially, captures China's rise as a global superpower and the implications of that development.

Stories of food are also stories of power. In LA's Koreatown, where most of the ethnic businesses and clientele are Korean, and where we may therefore have postulated the existence of a homogeneous ethnic population, class lines cut through ethnicity, distinguishing affluent Koreans from less well-to-do or even homeless Koreans. In Baltimore, the arrival of large-scale Korean supermarkets resulted in small ethnic groceries being squeezed out from street corners. The absence of Korean restaurants in Kona tells a story of the intersection between two colonizations and three waves of migration involving Japan's colonial administration stopping early Korean immigration to Hawai'i, Hawai'i's annexation to the United States (along with other factors), and Japanese colonialism pushing Koreans out of the peninsula toward the Japanese archipelago. Parts of this intersection are also evident in Japan in the form of strange incarnations of barbecued tripe, an absence of pears in meat marinade, and the use of the term *yakiniku,* or barbecued meat, as a synonym for Korean cuisine until very recent times. Meanwhile, the *galbi* (barbecued beef) that I found at a Vietnamese restaurant in Kona tells another, more recent story of immigration and uneven global power relations; while the use of the term *yakiniku* in Waikiki, in turn, signifies one of the strategies deployed by restaurateurs as they aggressively strive to respond to global market forces and the needs of the foreign tourists that such forces bring to Hawaiʻi's shores. The influx of affluent Chinese international students to the University of Iowa campus contrasts with the living conditions faced by long-term Asian migrants in Iowa, many of whom arrived as refugees during and after the Vietnam War. Similarly, changing U.S.–Korea trade relations have seen closer connections develop between meat and corn production in Iowa and the market for such products in Korea, with a direct impact on the lives of Korean producers and consumers. In sum, following the trajectories taken by certain examples of Korean food has revealed multiple nexuses involving unequal crisscrossings in international power relations as well as in U.S. domestic race relations.

Is Authentic Food Possible?

As I proposed in the Introduction, the stories told in this book are concerned, to a significant degree, with the notion of authenticity. Referring to the study of the invention of an authentic national cuisine in Belize presented by Richard Wilk (1999), Charles Lindholm convincingly proposes that a search by newly independent Belize for appropriate national symbols led to the creation of a completely invented dish known as "Royal Rat" (stuffed, roasted gibnut), the gibnut being "a shy, guinea-pig-like rodent who lives peacefully in the dense jungles of the tiny country of Belize" (Lindholm 2008: 77). Perhaps the example of the Belizean stuffed rodent is an extreme one, but this kind of phenomenon is widely recognizable in the world today—that is to say, a moment in which national authenticity is revealed as being based on a creation or invention. The example of the Korean government's effort to standardize *kimchi* is a case in point. Rather than allowing *kimchi* to continue to diversify naturally in an uncontrolled and almost amorphous fashion throughout the diverse regions of Korea, the government of South Korea sought to standardize it—thereby risking the impoverishment of its own cuisine—in order to use it as a definitive bearer of national authenticity. Considering that the key ingredient of *kimchi* is powdered chili pepper, a spice that originated in the New World, one can appreciate the difficulty of sustaining the integrity of any claim to authenticity in this case.

The pervasive assumption that supports such claims is that there can be only one form of national authenticity, the implication being that use of the plural form is in itself evidence of falsehood. This argument represents a considerable challenge when thinking about authenticity in our current postmodern, postindustrial, and globalizing world—a world in which supposedly authentic products are continually and continuously being invented, created, re-created, and reinvented in a competitive capitalist market where the need to distinguish one's products from those of one's rivals is indissolubly connected with the accumulation of profit and market share.

In the preceding chapters, we explored notions of authenticity in the context of four Korean food items at four different sites throughout the United States. The *naengmyeon* that we encountered in Los Angeles was similar to the North Korean version, which is arguably more authentic than that found in South Korea—especially the kind found in its food courts. But, it would nevertheless be difficult to deny the authentic status of South Korean *naengmyeon,* particularly given the modifications made to this traditional northern Korean delicacy by the current North Korean regime as it seeks to increase the share of the global market occupied by its version of this dish. After all, how can a traditional dish remain intact during a sixty-year period in which the nation has endured partition under rival regimes and a devastating civil war? This is a logical impossibility, and perhaps a historical impossibility too.

As we followed *jeon*'s metamorphosis from ceremonial food to global supermarket merchandise, we noticed an unmistakable process of secularization. When a ceremonial food becomes unceremonial, has it not lost its authenticity? In addition, the anomaly of having *jeon* (or any such dish) served as a main dish at Korean restaurants in the United States revealed a blatant modification in the way Korean food is served, again involving, as it were, a process of de-authentication. Strictly speaking, a side dish such as *jeon* could not possibly be served as a main dish, as I argued in Chapter 2; yet this has become the norm in both U.S. and South Korean restaurants.

Authenticity became a matter of visibility in Kona, Hawai'i, where Korean food was generally embedded in other foods or found at restaurants specializing in other kinds of cuisine. When Korean restaurants were found, they departed notably from the conventions found at Korean restaurants on the U.S. mainland. In stark contrast to its hidden status in Kona, Korean food in Honolulu maintained a high level of visibility, albeit largely subsumed under the term *yakiniku* as a marketing tool aimed at Japanese tourists. This same notion, that of visibility (or the lack thereof), was also a key to understanding the *yakiniku* barbecue in Japan, long believed to be practically the only authentic Korean dish in Japan. Our discussion of the invisibility of *yakiniku* as an ethnic (*esunikku*) food in Japan, tellingly capturing its colonial origins, also revealed that Japanese recipes for Korean barbecued meat digress from "authentic" Korean recipes that normally include pears. This makes it all the more intriguing, yet in retrospect wholly understandable, that *yakiniku* has come to gain currency as a synonym for Korean food in Waikiki, catering to the waves of Japanese tourists.

Finally, in our journey to America's heartland, we discovered *bibimbap* being enjoyed by international students from China, as if to reflect metaphorically the changing face of an internationalizing and diversifying campus. Closer consideration, however, led us to realize that "authentic *bibimbap*" is a contradiction in terms. For, *bibimbap* was originally a way of using any leftover dishes that a household could put its hands on, mixing everything together in an ersatz, ad hoc manner. The very nature of this dish defeats the seeming insistence on singularity inherent in the notion of authenticity.

As Lindholm argues, if a particular national cuisine can be or tends to be an invention yet its effects are real, then we can say that we have lost the nature or original state with which authenticity identifies itself. For, if that national cuisine is an invention, there can be no natural state to which that invention can return; rather, it would have to continue inventing and reinventing itself as a new, even more authentic national cuisine. However, if we were to conceive of the natural state of national cuisine as an ongoing process of invention and reinvention of itself, then the state of nature itself would be transformed. That is to say that the natural state of national cuisine entails, perhaps necessarily, a state of constant self-invention and reinvention. By adopting this approach we can grasp national cuisine as something that evolves and changes through time and space: time, because it lives in history while itself participating in the making of history; and space, because it travels transnationally, just as people do. Seen in this way, there is nothing inauthentic about Korean national cuisine becoming a global phenomenon on the world stage, be it in the United States or Japan.

On the other hand, if the authenticity of a particular national cuisine has to be situated in relation to others—in dialogue with them in an environment characterized by diversity and difference—then the entire meaning of the authenticity itself changes. It changes from a set of unchangeable attributes to a quality that is not only defined from within itself (its own evolution and transformation) but also by the intervention and influence of others from the outside. Thus, once a Korean dish—such as *naengmyeon* or *jeon*—travels beyond Korea's national boundaries, its authenticity changes in accordance with what others define it to be. In this way of thinking, the *jeon* or *naengmyeon* found at any Korean restaurant in the United States or elsewhere is as authentic as any *jeon* or *naengmyeon* found in restaurants in Korea itself. This approach also reveals the impossibility of using the concept of unity when discussing national cuisine, because, as Mintz has suggested (see Introduction), there is a pronounced diversity in regional cuisines. So, if an example of *bibimbap* in Jeonju, Korea, were different from one found in Seoul, each would nevertheless retain its integrity as an authentic regional dish of Korea.

If the above analysis enables us to continue using the term "authenticity" when talking about diverse reincarnations of Korean food items in time and space, how are we to understand the finding of this book that many of the food items we encountered and the symbolic meanings they represent came about almost by coincidence or through some sort of historical accident? Take, for instance, the case of *horumon yaki* (barbecued tripe), a dish that came to be an important part of the *yakiniku* (barbecued meat) menu, which, in turn became synonymous with Korean cuisine in Japan. Poverty-stricken Korean colonial immigrants to Japan took advantage of traditional Japanese practices of meat consumption, in which organs were largely discarded. Furthermore, a lack of resources led colonial immigrants to go without using pears in their marinade sauce, this pearless version in turn becoming the standard (or indeed, authentic) form of Korean-style barbecue sauce as understood in Japan. And take, for instance, the example of *naengmyeon,* a northern delicacy, which was brought to the south as millions of refugees fled from the north during the Korean War, subsequently becoming a food-court favorite not only in Seoul but also in Los Angeles' Koreatown.

What all this tells us is that, when a food item—whether considered part of a national cuisine or not—travels transnationally and transhistorically, there is usually a story attached to it, a story of colonialism, immigration, an oppressive domestic polity, an international market characterized by uneven power relations, stark divisions in ideology (as in the case of the Cold War), and so on. Realizing this, one begins to understand that the discovery of authentic-tasting *galbi* at a Vietnamese restaurant in Kona or the sight of a beautiful range of variety packs containing *jeon* at a Baltimore supermarket cannot simply be written off with innocence or simple curiosity. Likewise, whether they are found in Los Angeles, Baltimore, Kona, or Iowa City, dishes such as *naengmyeon, jeon, galbi,* and *bibimbap* all tell stories of Korea's colonial history, its partition, the dispersion of Koreans, and their migration in the context of today's globalizing world, a world in which the notion of authenticity as it relates to national identity—and as it is embodied in food—constantly transforms itself in new and creative ways while still retaining its integrity.

Authenticity and Capitalism

Before closing this volume let us ask one last time, what *is* authenticity? Among philosophers who have examined the notion of authenticity, one of the most often cited is Jean-Jacques Rousseau. Rousseau proposed that authenticity could be summarized as a return to nature, arguing that it is only in nature that true self can manifest itself and that, conversely, true self is already there, naturally existent, not needing to be made, created, or invented, let alone fabricated. Based on the reading of Rousseau's novels, notably *Emile* and *New Heloise,* Alessandro Ferrara proposes that Rousseau's concept of the social contract involves not only autonomy, but also authenticity and empathy, self-knowledge and the capacity to accept one's true self as it is, that is, one's inner nature, and that these attributes are "indispensable for the emancipation of social relations" (Ferrara 1993: 27).

Throughout this book, I have, as a working concept, understood the meaning of authenticity as (1) being true to the original, and (2) being at one with the original. According to this understanding, authentic qualities are no longer authentic once they have been separated (alienated) from the original. Being at one with the original overlaps with Rousseau's notion of a return to nature, that is, a state in which nothing is artificially masked. However, the act of cooking is not quite natural, as it involves skill, effort, and, ultimately, art. As such, every act of cooking is a reproduction of some sort. In order to consider this question, I turn to Walter Benjamin who, when exploring the meaning of art and the implications of mechanical reproduction, wrote: "One might generalize by saying: the technique of reproduction detaches the reproduced object from the domain of tradition. By making many reproductions it substitutes a plurality of copies for a unique existence. And in permitting the reproduction to meet the beholder or listener in his own particular situation, it reactivates the object reproduced" (Benjamin 2010: 14). With particular emphasis on film and the fundamental differences between it and theater, Benjamin notes that the reproducibility of film invites the liquidation of the authenticity of tradition and culture (2010: 14–15).

Benjamin is not, however, referring to reproducibility in general. The traditional, manual copying of a masterpiece, for example, has a meaning—whether it is carried out for the purpose of study and training on one hand or as forgery on the other—quite different from the case of mechanized mass reproduction, in which it becomes easy to claim that a copy is identical to (or at one with) the original. Needless to say, Benjamin points us to the capitalist mode of production itself, which presupposes mass production, and therefore mass reproduction of one commodity after another, each replica in turn claiming authenticity.

In the foregoing discussion, I have noted several times that the act of cooking involves the reproduction, mimicking, or copying of an original recipe. If, as is insisted in cooking recipes, in restaurants, and on the labels of supermarket foods, every meal that is created is an authentic one, then the original is reproduced every time—a contradiction in terms. For, if the original can be re-created and re-presented every time, then the original—the natural state—is no longer original. Placing this inquiry in the national scale augments the problem. For, how can a food item claim national authenticity given the further contradiction between this notion and the way in which modern nation-states have come into existence—that is to say, far from naturally? And, how does national authenticity play out in the context of globalization, a context in which we might even talk of something called "global authenticity"? For example, at one of the countless stores in the global network of franchised restaurants controlled by McDonald's, where mechanically reproduced copies of its authentic recipes are delivered to stores in identical packaging in frozen form accompanied by uniform instructions that employees must follow with minimal individual input—placing a frozen packet into a microwave, for example—every single combo or meal can be considered authentic. The capitalist mechanism ensures that even the potatoes used for McDonald's French fries are identical, according to Wenonah Hauter:

> Three large companies, ConAgra, McCain Foods, and J. R. Simplot, manufacture the enormous number of fries sold by McDonald's. These companies use the required russet potatoes produced by the giant United Fresh Potato Growers of Idaho. Bayer CropScience and Monsanto provide the specified seeds, herbicides, and pesticides for the contract farmers who produce the potatoes, which then become the uniform size and shape of fries consumed at McDonald's and other chains. (Hauter 2012: 68)

This leads us to think about authenticity under current historical conditions, that is to say, authenticity in the age of global capitalism. For, my journey across the United States following the trajectories taken by Korean food was also a journey following in the giant footsteps of global capitalism. Accordingly, my search for authenticity took place within the confines of this political-economic system. A logical question to ask, therefore, would be: Is authentic food possible in capitalism? This question may best be addressed by asking another question: What does it mean to eat in capitalist society?

In capitalism, almost everything is mediated by money, and is therefore replaceable by it. The young Marx wrote:

> What I as a man cannot do, i.e. what all my individual powers cannot do, I can do with the help of *money.* Money therefore transforms each of these essential powers into something which it is not, into its *opposite.*
>
> If I desire a meal or want to take the mail coach because I am not strong enough to make the journey on foot, money can procure me both the meal and the mail coach, i.e. it transfers my wishes from the realm of imagination, it translates them from their existence as thought, imagination and desires into their *sensuous, real* existence, from imagination into life, and from imagined being into real being. In this mediating role money is the *truly creative* power. . . . If I have no money for travel, I have no *need,* i.e. no real and self-realizing need, to travel. . . . *Money,* which is the external, universal *means* and *power*—derived not from man as man and not from human society as society—to turn *imagination into reality and reality into mere imagination . . .* [M]oney is the universal inversion of *individualities,* which it turns into their opposites and to whose qualities it attaches contradictory qualities. (Marx 1992 [1844]: 378; emphases in original)

From the above, it should be clear to us that under the capitalist regime of money as an agent of generalized exchange, nothing remains irreplaceable and everything becomes exchangeable, with money playing a key role in enabling this infinite reproduction, as it is virtually exchangeable with just about anything. This in itself makes it impossible for anything to remain authentic.

If, along with all other human activities in capitalism, eating is made possible by money, how can we begin to understand the act of eating in the age of capitalism, let alone eating authentic food? For it appears that eating can be replaced by other acts so long as one has the money to pay for it. Furthermore, if almost everything can be replaced with other things via the power of money, can any one thing still be authentic and remain so? Or can authenticity also be reduced to a matter of payment? Lionel Trilling sums it up for us as follows: "Money, in short, is the principle of the inauthentic in human existence" (Trilling 1972: 124).

Let us think about this question by taking a brief detour using a simplified—and I emphasize "simplified"—example. If a worker has to eat supper in order to return to the factory the next day, his act of eating does not contribute to the growth of his own human self but rather to the profit making of the capitalist. In this case, food for the worker is an integral part of capitalism that bypasses the overall process of the worker's own human re-creation (which has now become irrelevant to his act of eating). In other words, the act of eating here is not done for the worker's well-being, even though it is the worker himself who has carried out the act: he eats for the capitalist; the capitalist eats for him. When the worker is laid off, does he eat for himself? No, because now his entire existence is oriented toward the goal of obtaining gainful employment. He eats as a reserve for the capitalist who will employ him in the future. What will happen if the worker ends up unable to find a job? He will have to go hungry, and if he can find food that he is able to afford, that food will be low-quality, highly processed, mass-produced food with minimal nutritional value, the long-term consumption of which is likely to result in deterioration of his health in the form of the possible onset of obesity, diabetes, and heart problems. Whether or not he has access to health care, the act of eating at this point is subordinate to his survival as a living being in the short term, even if it results in long-term harm, a state of affairs far removed from socially meaningful self-re-creation. Thus, even though he may be eating food, its consumption is external to him—estranged or alienated from him.

The anthropology of food cannot overlook this aspect of eating. In the final analysis, the nutritious, exciting, and beautiful creations that we admire on the tables of restaurants need to be understood as part of the same continuum that includes the alienation of workers from their food in capitalist society. At the same time, the items we purchase in Korean and other restaurants that claim authenticity for their food the money is eating for us; that is, we purchase authenticity and the power of money makes it authentic, thus rendering the authentic food replaceable. This has been a fundamental constraint that I have faced throughout my study; for authenticity and capitalism contradict each other.

Eating Authentically

Fully accepting that there are constraints and limitations when investigating authenticity in capitalism, and trying not to assume that everything simply succumbs to the logic of capitalism, we can draw upon the findings of this book to make the following assertions. We, as humans in the twenty-first century, eat in a diverse range of situations under varying conditions, sometimes involving what seem to be relatively individualistic choices, sometimes in response to market pressure, sometimes deploying knowledge and information in an attempt to achieve and maintain good health and minimize environmental damage, but also within the clear economic constraints of one's own limited means.

At the beginning of this volume, I noted the existence of a vast disparity between overeaters and hungry humans, in addition to the massive variation in the quality of food throughout the world, depending on the availability of resources, information, and technology. Weaving through this fabric, claims of authenticity assert themselves in relation to particular foods or entire cuisines. In this context, food items do not make themselves available to consumers in innocent or innocuous ways. Rather, they bear identities, brand names, signatures, standards, and—to use an unusual turn of phrase—authorships. Any of these can, of course, be removed from the actual ingredients or outcomes of eating that particular food, but in the global capitalist market, food items are, after all, commodities for circulation.

One eats because one is hungry, but more often than not one eats not simply because of hunger but because of habit, convention, a need for socialization, or in accordance with ritual rules or established practices on particular occasions, and so on—that is to say, one eats socially. The social aspect of eating makes the act more complicated than may be understood from the aforementioned story of the worker and the capitalist. Sociality and social relations accompany not only wealthy people eating plentiful quantities of gourmet food but also poor people eating lesser amounts at soup kitchens or charity outlets. In sum, eating happens in society even when one is eating alone and feels as if one is eating purely to fill one's stomach.

If we were to rely on Rousseau's conception of authenticity—being truthful to one's self—how would it be possible for us to eat authentically in capitalist society? Given the massive amount of aggressive marketing, lobbying, and attempts at policy manipulation on the part of corporate entities involved in the manufacture and retail of food products, it would be futile to insist on our ability to make choices removed from the effects and constraints of the capitalist economy and the global market. Yet, if we were to think about authenticity in connection with social relations on one hand and the self on the other, we would realize that eating authentically can happen rather unexpectedly, perhaps even paradoxically, if we take advantage of the capitalist logic of plurality and reproducibility. A mother can claim authenticity for a particular dish that she cooks, but this claim may well not be validated outside her immediate family. In fact, her mother-in-law may not accept the authenticity of her daughter-in-law's version, countering that her own recipe is more authentic. The Korean government's claiming the right to determine the authenticity of *kimchi* is an example of a claim to national authenticity being made in the international sphere, in spite of the fact that this authority has not been validated in Korea itself, where the *kimchi* market is filled with a vast range of different recipes. The Korean government may assert its authority in different ways at the domestic level, through the standardization of production criteria, for example, but it is unable to impose regulations regarding taste and ingredients, as evidenced by the huge variety of *kimchi* versions found on the shelves of supermarkets in Seoul (see Introduction).

In this context, not entirely unlike the possibility of the mechanical reproduction of art (according to Benjamin), we may postulate a multiplication in the authenticity—or, should one say, authority—of food. One may call it alienation from the original, but, after all, there is no clear reason why only the original version of a particular food or cuisine should be considered authentic, as, unlike art, food is perishable and meant to be consumed, the only permanent element (if any) confined within the form of the recipe itself. In this age of global capitalism, each quality that is inalienable from the original has become replicable and reproducible without losing its particular claim to authenticity, thus transforming the meaning of authenticity from one of singularity to one involving multiple singularities—the irreplaceable being replaced by the infinitely replaceable, creation replaced by endless re-creation—for as long as market demand continues to exist.

The Korean food items that I discussed in this volume followed this trajectory in their assertions of authenticity. *Yakiniku* remained a shorthand expression for Korean food in Japan from colonial times right up until the influx of South Korean immigrants to Japan from the late 1980s, yet it re-emerged in Honolulu as the name used for Korean food in marketing it to visiting Japanese tourists. Here, the authenticity of *yakiniku* goes through multiple shifts. When *jeon* doubles its role—no longer being simply a form of ritual food but also a supermarket commodity and a main dish served at Korean restaurants, no longer an example of food for the ancestors but a global food commodity—its authenticity is inevitably readjusted. Seen in this way, authenticity ceases to be a singular quality, itself becoming reproducible. Perhaps the authenticity of food has always existed in this way—in its potential to be reproduced. Yet, this potential has no doubt been intensified in the age of globalization and global capitalism.

Under these conditions, the eater faces a few constraints, including what kind of claims to authenticity one is subjected to and hence under what authority one is placed. Besides, with the exception of infancy and in advanced age, most human beings are not only consumers of food, but also producers, sellers, and preparers of it. In this sense, the process of eating would involve authenticity being found in and conferred upon food in multiple ways. A dilemma persists, though, due to the systemic constraints imposed by global capitalism on one's stomach. The lucrative nature of food as a basic element for the preservation of human life on this planet and its limitless potential to be harnessed in the generation of profits for the benefit of global capitalist forces can only be considered a tragedy. When thinking about Korean food in the United States and elsewhere one cannot escape this sense.

References

Abelmann, Nancy, and John Lie. 1997. *Blue Dreams: Korean Americans and the Los Angeles Riots*. Cambridge, MA: Harvard University Press.

Akiyama, Noriko. 2013. "Passion for Hawaii: With Numbers in Decline, Tour Operators Try to Lure Japanese Tourists Back." *Asahi Shimbun,* July 28, 2013. Online: http://ajw.asahi.com/article/globe/feature/hawaii/AJ201307280013 (accessed December 25, 2013).

Albritton, Robert. 2009. *Let Them Eat Junk: How Capitalism Creates Hunger and Obesity*. London: Pluto Press.

Allen, Helena. 1982. *The Betrayal of Liliuokalani: Last Queen of Hawaii 1838–1917*. Honolulu: Mutual Publishing.

"A Look at Iowa Agriculture." 2010. Online: www.agclassroom.org/ia (accessed April 27, 2012).

Anderson, Jay, and Candace Matelic. 1980. *Living History Farms: A Pictorial History of Food in Iowa*. Des Moines, IA: The Living History Farms Foundation.

Anderson, Joseph L. 2009. *Industrializing the Corn Belt: Agriculture, Technology, and Environment, 1945–1972*. DeKalb: University of Northern Illinois Press.

Bak, Sangmee. 2010. "Exoticizing the Familiar, Domesticating the Foreign: Ethnic Food Restaurants in Korea." *Korea Journal* 50 (1): 110–132.

Bakalar, Nicholas. 2008. "Nutrition: MSG Use Is Linked to Obesity." *New York Times,* August 26, 2008. Online: http://www.nytimes.com/2008/08/26/health/nutrition/26nutr.html (accessed February 21, 2012).

"Beef Farmers Full of Worry over Future." 2007. *The Hankyoreh,* May 31, 2007. Online: http://english.hani.co.kr/arti/english_edition/e_entertainment/213049.html (accessed April 27, 2012).

Benjamin, Walter. 2010. *The Work of Art in the Age of Mechanical Reproduction*. Scottsdale, AZ: Prism Key Press.

Berthelsen, John. 2011. "South Korea's Food Security Alarm." *Asia Sentinel,* April 30, 2011. Online: http://farmlandgrab.org/post/view/18525 (accessed February 12, 2012).

Bestor, Ted. 2004. *Tsukiji: The Fish Market at the Center of the World*. Berkeley: University of California Press.

————. 2005. "How Sushi Went Global." In J. Watson and M. Caldwell, eds., *The Cultural Politics of Food and Eating: A Reader,* 13–20. New York: Blackwell.

Bower, Anne, ed. 1997. *Recipes for Reading: Community Cookbooks, Stories, Histories.* Amherst: University of Massachusetts Press.

Brewington, Kelly. 2007. "Korean-Americans Burdened with Guilt, Shame and Fear of Backlash: Virginia Tech Shootings." *Baltimore Sun,* April 21, 2007. Online: http://articles.baltimoresun.com/2007–04–21/news/0704210128_1_korean-american-co alition-korean-community-korean-americans (accessed March 1, 2012).

Brown, Felicity. 2009. "Meat Consumption Per Capita." *The Guardian,* September 2, 2009. Online: http://www.guardian.co.uk/environment/datablog/2009/sep/02/meat-consumption-per-capita-climate-change (accessed March 22, 2012).

"Cabbage Shortage Leaves Koreans Hungry for Kimchi." 2010. *CNN World,* October 5, 2010. Online: http://articles.cnn.com/2010–10–05/world/skorea.kimchi.short age_1_cabbage-shortage-korean-families-south-koreans?_s=PM:WORLD (accessed February 25, 2012).

Carlson, Tucker. 1995. "Bigotry in Baltimore." *City Journal,* Autumn 1995. Online: http://www.city-journal.org/html/5_4_sndgs01.html (accessed February 28, 2012).

Carson, Larry. 2007. "Health Violations Close Ellicott City Supermarket: Inspectors Find Rodent Infestation, Thawed Food, Dripping Water." *Baltimore Sun,* August 10, 2007. Online: http://articles.baltimoresun.com/2007–08–10/news/0708100141_1 _store-closed-food-packaging-lotte-plaza (accessed March 1, 2012).

Chang, Edward Taehan. 2003. "Korean Americans" *Asian-Nation: The Landscape of Asian America.* Online: http://www.asian-nation.org/korean.shtml (accessed March 6, 2012).

Choe, Sang-Hun. 2008. "Protests in Seoul More about Nationalism than U.S. Beef." *The New York Times,* June 11, 2008. Online: http://www.nytimes.com/2008/06/11/world /asia/11iht-seoul.1.13635643.html?_r=1 (accessed April 27, 2012).

Choi, Eun-hui, Jun-hui Kim, Bong-hui O, Yeong-hui Yi, Ji-yeon Yi, and Gyeong-sun Han. 2007. *Hanguk eumsiggui ihae* [Understanding Korean food]. Seoul: MU Midieo.

Chun, Jaewoon Lee, and Youngran Baek. 2004. *Authentic Recipes from Korea.* Singapore: Periplus.

Chung, Seung-mo. 2006. *Markets: Traditional Korean Society.* Seoul: Ewha Womans University Press.

"Cities with the Highest Percentages of Asians in Iowa." N.d. Online: http://zipatlas .com/us/ia/city-comparison/percentage-asian-population.htm (accessed April 5, 2012).

Civitello, Linda. 2008. *Cuisine and Culture: A History of Food and People.* New York: Wiley.

Codex Stan 223. 2001. *Codex Standard for Kimchi (Codes Stan 223–2001).* Online: www .codexalimentarius.net/download/standards/365/CXS_223e.pdf (accessed February 25, 2012).

Coffman, Tom. 2009. *Nation Within: The History of the American Occupation of Hawai'i.* Kihei, HI: Koa Books.

Counihan, Carole. 1999. *The Anthropology of Food and Body: Gender, Meaning, Power.* New York: Routledge.

Counihan, Carole, and Steven Kaplan, eds. 1998. *Food and Gender: Identity and Power.* London: Taylor & Francis.

Croucher, Martin, and Carol Huang. 2010. "North Korea Serves up Everything but Politics in Deira." *The National,* December 14, 2010. Online: http://www.thenational .ae/news/world/asia-pacific/n-korea-serves-up-everything-but-politics-in-deira (accessed February 16, 2012).

Davidson, Osha Gray. 1996. *Broken Heartland: The Rise of America's Rural Ghetto.* Iowa City: University of Iowa Press.

Dean, Stacy, and Dottie Rosenbaum. 2013. "SNAP Benefits Will Be Cut for All Participants in November 2013." *Center on Budget and Policy Priorities.* Online: www .cbpp.org/cms/?fa=views&id=3899 (accessed December 1, 2013).

"Demographic Statistics: Hawaii." 2000. *Infoplease.* Online: http://www.infoplease.com /us/census/data/hawaii/demographic.html (accessed September 11, 2014).

Derr, Mark. 1997. *Dog's Best Friend: Annals of the Dog-Human Relationship.* New York: Henry Holt & Co.

Douglas, Mary. 1966. *Purity and Danger: An Analysis of the Concepts of Pollution and Taboo.* New York: Routledge.

———. 1972. "Deciphering a Meal." *Daedalus* 1 (101): 61–81.

Engdahl, William. 2007. *Seeds of Destruction: The Hidden Agenda of Genetic Manipulation.* New York: Global Research.

Fabiosa, Jacinto F., Dermot J. Hayes, and Fengxia Dong. 2007. "Impact of the South Korea–U.S. Free Trade Agreement on the U.S. Livestock Sector." *Working Paper* 07-WP 455. November 2007. Online: http://ageconsearch.umn.edu/bitstream/7701/1 /wp070455.pdf (accessed April 27, 2012).

Fabrizio, Kerry, Rajesh Potineni, and Kim Gray. 2010. "Instant Noodle Seasonings." In G. G. Hou, ed., *Asian Noodles: Science, Technology, and Processing,* 141–163. Hoboken, NJ: Wiley.

Ferrara, Alessandro. 1993. *Modernity and Authenticity: A Study of the Social and Ethical Thought of Jean-Jacques Rousseau.* Albany: SUNY Press.

"Fifa Warns S Korea over Dog Meat." 2001. *BBC News,* November 6, 2001. Online: http:// news.bbc.co.uk/2/hi/asia-pacific/1640848.stm (accessed March 29, 2012).

Food Research and Action Center. 2013. "Hunger in America, 2013." In Peter Pringle, ed., *A Place at the Table: The Crisis of 49 Million Hungry Americans and How to Solve It.* New York: PublicAffairs.

Freedman, Paul. 2008. *Out of the East: Spices and the Medieval Imagination.* New Haven, CT: Yale University Press.

Freeman, Matthew. 2006. "Reconsidering the Effects of Monosodium Glutamate: A Literature Review." *Journal of the American Academy of Nurse Practitioners* 18: 482–486.

Gabaccia, Donna. 1998. *We Are What We Eat.* Cambridge, MA: Harvard University Press.

Gliona, John. 2010. "Kimchi Crisis Leaves South Koreans Hot Under the Collar." *Los Angeles Times,* October 5, 2010. Online: http://articles.latimes.com/2010/oct/05 /world/la-fg-south-korea-kimchi-20101005 (accessed February 25, 2012).

Goody, Jack. 1982. *Cooking, Cuisine and Class: A Study in Comparative Sociology.* Cambridge: Cambridge University Press.

———. 1998. "The Globalization of Chinese Food." In J. Goody, *Food and Love: A Cultural History of East and West,* 161–170. London: Verso.

"Great Leader, but Even Better Noodles." 1999. *Newsweek,* May 16, 1999. Online: http://www.thedailybeast.com/newsweek/1999/05/16/great-leader-but-even-better-noodles.html (accessed February 16, 2012).

Ham, Yeong. 2010. *Inyeoneuro babeul jitta: Seunimdeului jayeon bapsang bibeop* [Cooking rice with relationships: Secret recipe of natural diet of the monks]. Seoul: Time Popular Books.

Han, Bok-jin. 2009. *Uri eumsigui maseul mannada* [Meeting the flavor of our own food]. Seoul: Seoul National University Press.

Han, Bok-ryeo. 2004. *Jibeseo mandeuneun gungjung eumsik* [Royal cuisine that you can cook at home]. Seoul: Cheongrim.

Han, Kyung-Koo. 2010. "Noodle Odyssey: East Asia and Beyond." *Korea Journal* 50 (1): 60–84.

Harvey, David. 1990. *The Condition of Postmodernity: An Enquiry into the Origins of Cultural Change.* Oxford: Blackwell.

———. 2005. *A Brief History of Neoliberalism.* Oxford: Oxford University Press.

Hauter, Wenonah. 2012. *Foodopoly: The Battle over the Future of Food and Farming in America.* New York: The New Press.

Hazama, Dorothy Ochiai, and Jane Okamoto Komeiji. 1986. *The Japanese in Hawai'i Okage Sama De.* Honolulu: Bess Press.

Helstosky, Carol. 2003. "Recipe for the Nation: Reading Italian History through La Scienza in Cucina and La Cucina Futurista." *Food and Foodways* 11 (2): 113–140.

Hepinstall, Hi Soo Shin. 2001. *Growing Up in a Korean Kitchen: A Cookbook.* Berkeley: Ten Speed Press.

Hirayama, T. 1987. "Epidemiology of Breast Cancer with Special Reference to the Role of Diet." *Preventive Medicine* 7: 173–195.

Hoeffel, Elizabeth, Sonya Rastogi, Myoung Ouk Kim, and Hasan Shahid. 2012. *The Asian Population: 2010.* Online: http://www.census.gov/prod/cen2010/briefs/c2010br-11.pdf (accessed December 25, 2013).

Howard County Maryland Economic Development Authority. 2011a. "Demographics: Howard County." Online: http://www.hceda.org/demographics.aspx?details=howard (accessed March 6, 2012).

———. 2011b. "Demographics: Ellicott City." Online: http://www.hceda.org/demographics.aspx?details=ellicott (accessed March 6, 2012).

Hwang, Young-jin. 2007. "Beef Sales Bring Out a Storm of Protests." *JoongAng Daily,* July 14, 2007. Online: http://koreajoongangdaily.joinsmsn.com/news/article/article.aspx?aid=2878042 (accessed April 27, 2012).

Inglis, David, and Debra Gimlin, eds. 2009. *The Globalization of Food.* Oxford: Berg.

Iowa Department of Public Health. 2010. "Table 16: Leading Causes of Death by Selected Age Groups," *Vital Statistics of Iowa, 2010.* Online: http://www.idph.state.ia.us/apl/vital_stats.asp (accessed April 28, 2012).

James, Michael. 1997. "Crime Grips Korean Merchants Slayings, Robberies Unsettle Community." *Baltimore Sun,* January 29, 1997. Online: http://articles.baltimoresun

.com/1997–01–29/news/1997029033_1_korean-community-korean-american-mer
chants (accessed March 1, 2012).

James, Michael, and Norris West. 1995. "Jurors Defend Verdict in Slaying of Student."
Baltimore Sun, August 2, 1995. Online: http://articles.baltimoresun.com/1995-08-02
/news/1995214049_1_deliberations-verdict-korean-community (accessed September
14, 2014).

"Japan Korea Kimchi Dispute." 2001. *Ted Case Studies,* January 2001. Online: http://
www1.american.edu/ted/kimchi.htm (accessed February 25, 2012).

Jo, Hu-jong. 2001. *Uri eumsik iyagi* [Stories of our food]. Seoul: Hollym.

Jones, Martin. 2007. *Feast: Why Humans Share Food.* Oxford: Oxford University Press.

Ju, Jin Soon. 2000. "Nutrition in the Republic of Korea." *British Journal of Nutrition*
84: Supplement 2: S195–S198.

June, Audrey Williams. 2010. "U. of Iowa Lists 14 Graduate Programs at Risk for Cuts
or Elimination." *Chronicle of Higher Education,* February 17, 2010. Online: http://
chronicle.com/article/U-of-Iowa-Lists-14-Graduat/64229/ (accessed April 5, 2012).

Kazuko, Emi, and Young Jin Song. 2010. *The Food and Cooking of Japan and Korea.*
London: Lorenze Books/Annes Publishing.

Keene, Danya, Mark Padilla, and Arline Geronimus. 2010. "Leaving Chicago for Iowa's 'Fields of Opportunity': Community Dispossession, Rootlessness, and the Quest
for Somewhere to 'Be OK.'" *Human Organization* 69 (3): 275–284.

Kendall, Laurel. 2009. "Korean Shamanism and the Spirits of Capitalism." In L. Kendall, *Shamans, Nostalgias, and the IMF: South Korean Popular Religion in Motion,*
129–153. Honolulu: University of Hawai'i Press.

Kenner, Robert. 2009. *Food, Inc.* Film. DVD.

Kenyon, Peter. 2010. "Dubai Restaurant Offers a Taste of North Korea." *NPR,* December 31, 2010. Online: http://www.npr.org/2010/12/31/132491605/dubai-restaurant-
offers-a-taste-of-north-korea (accessed February 16, 2012).

Kim, Chan-jeong. 1982. *Chōsenjin jokōno uta: 1930nen kishiwada bōseki sōgi* [Songs
of Korean female factory workers: The 1930 labor dispute in Kishiwada textile in-
dustry]. Tokyo: Iwanami shoten.

Kim, Elaine. 1996. "Appendix A." In Elaine Kim and Eui-young Yu, eds., *East to America: Korean American Life Stories.* New York: The New Press.

Kim, Eun-hui, and Hye-ok Jeong. 2002. *Hangukeumsik* [Korean food]. Seoul: Munjisa.

Kim, Hyun Ja, Woong Ki Chang, Mi Kyung Kim, Sang Sun Lee, and Bo Youl Choi.
2002. "Dietary Factors and Gastric Cancer in Korea: A Case-Control Study." *International Journal of Cancer* 97 (4): 531–535.

Kim, In-ku. 1999. "NK Restaurant Denies Connection to Seoul Outlet." *The Chosun
Ilbo,* June 13, 1999. Online: http://english.chosun.com/site/data/html_dir/1999
/06/13/1999061361287.html (accessed February 16, 2012).

Kim, Kwang Ok. 2010. "Rice Cuisine and Cultural Practice in Contemporary Korean
Dietary Life." *Korea Journal* 50 (1): 12–35.

Kim, Myeong-hui, Ji-yeong Han, and Jin-yeong Kim. 2005. *Jeontong Hanguk eumsik*
[Traditional Korean cuisine]. Seoul: Kwangmoonkag.

Kim, Nadia. 2008. *Imperial Citizens: Koreans and Race from Seoul to LA.* Stanford, CA:
Stanford University Press.

Kim, Ok-kyeong. 2009. *Naruel sallin jayeonsik bapsang* [The natural foods table that healed me]. Seoul: Dongnyeok.

Kim, Seon-mi. 2010. *Saengmyeongeul guhago jigureul sallineun sallimui bapsang* [Life table that saves lives and heals the earth]. Seoul: Dongnyeok.

Kim, Yeong-dal. 1996. "Hoshō: Kaisetsuto tōkeino hosoku" [Supplementary chapter: Additional explanation on statistics]. In Morita Yoshio, *Sūjiga kataru zainichi kankoku chōsenjinno rekishi* [History of Koreans in Japan told by statistics]. Tokyo: Akashi shoten.

Kim, Yun-seon, and Yong-jong Yi. 2010. *Hanguginui chejire manneun yakseon bapsang* [Medicinal diet that goes well with the physical build of Koreans]. Seoul: Moabooks.

Kimbrell, Andrew, ed. 2002. *The Fatal Harvest Reader: The Tragedy of Industrial Agriculture*. New York: Island Press.

Kimura, Yukiko. 1988. *Issei: Japanese Immigrants in Hawaii*. Honolulu: University of Hawai'i Press.

Kirk, Don. 1999. "Restaurateur Turns North Korean Recipe into Hot Ticket in Seoul: Melting a Cold War with Cold Noodles." *New York Times,* May 22, 1999. Online: http://www.nytimes.com/1999/05/22/business/worldbusiness/22iht-noodle.2.t.html?pagewanted=1 (accessed February 16, 2012).

"Kitachōsen resutoran chūgokuni 60 ten gaika kakutoku, jōhōshūshūkyoten? Kankoku seifu, riyōjishukuo yōsei" [North Korean restaurants—sixty of them in China, for foreign currency, intelligence gathering? South Korean government is requesting restraint (of its citizens) on using these restaurants]. 2010. *Sankei nyūsu,* June 26, 2010. Online: http://sankei.jp.msn.com/affairs/news/110121/crm11012112510201-n1.htm (accessed February 16, 2012).

Kohatsu, Kimberly. 2012. "Why Do Hawaiians Love Spam So Much?" *Huffington Post,* September 24, 2012. Online: http://www.huffingtonpost.com/Menuism/why-do-hawaiians-love-spam-so-much_b_1901306.html (accessed December 25, 2013).

Krimmel, Dean. 2004. "A Timeline of Baltimore's Immigration." *Urbanite,* May 1, 2004. Online: http://www.urbanitebaltimore.com/baltimore/a-timeline-of-baltimores-immigration/Content?oid=1244571 (accessed March 1, 2012).

Kurihara, Kenzo. 2009. "Glutamate: From Discovery as a Food Flavor to Role as a Basic Taste (Umami)." *American Journal of Clinical Nutrition* 90 (Suppl.): 719S–722S.

Lankov, Andrei. 2007. *North of the DMZ: Essays on Daily Life in North Korea*. Jefferson, NC: McFarland.

Lee, Cecilia Hae-Jin. 2009. *Quick & Easy Korean Cooking*. San Francisco: Chronicle Books.

Lee, Hyuk-Joon, Han-Kwang Yang, and Yoon-Ok Ahn. 2002. "Gastric Cancer in Korea." *Gastric Cancer* 5: 177–182.

Lee, Min-June, Barry Popkin, and Soowon Kim. 2002. "The Unique Aspects of the Nutrition Transition in South Korea: The Retention of Healthful Elements in Their Traditional Diet." *Public Health Nutrition* 5 (1A): 197–203.

Lee, Sandra Soo-Jin. 2000. "Dys-Appearing Tongues and Bodily Memories: The Aging of First-Generation Resident Koreans in Japan." *Ethos* 28 (2): 198–223.

Levinstein, Harvey. 2003a. *Paradox of Plenty: A Social History of Eating in Modern America*. Berkeley: University of California Press.

———. 2003b. *Revolution at the Table: The Transformation of the American Diet*. Berkeley: University of California Press.

Lévi-Strauss, Claude. 1964. *Les Mythologiques: L'Origine des manières de table*. Paris: Plon.

Lien, Marianne Elisabeth. 2009. "Standards, Science and Scale: The Case of Tasmanian Atlantic Salmon." In D. Inglis and D. Gimlin, eds., 65–80. *The Globalization of Food*. Oxford: Berg.

Lili'uokalani. 1898. *Hawaii's Story by Hawaii's Queen*. Boston: Lothrop, Lee and Shepherd.

Lindemann, Bernd, Yoko Ogiwara, and Yuzo Ninomiya. 2002. "The Discovery of Umami." *Chemical Senses* 27: 843–844.

Lindholm, Charles. 2008. *Culture and Authenticity*. Oxford: Blackwell.

MacDonald, Heather. 1995. "Why Koreans Succeed." *City Journal*, Spring 1995. Online: http://www.city-journal.org/html/5_2_a2.html (accessed Feburary 28, 2012).

Marcus, George. 1995. "Ethnography in/of the World System: The Emergence of Multi-Sited Ethnography." *Annual Review of Anthropology* 24: 95–117.

Marx, Karl. 1992 [1844]. "Economic and Philosophical Manuscripts (1844)." In Karl Marx, *Early Writings*, 279–400. New York: Penguin and New Left Review.

McNally, David. 2006. *Another World Is Possible: Globalization and Anti-Capitalism*. Monmouth: Merlin Press.

Mintz, Sidney. 1985. *Sweetness and Power: The Place of Sugar in Modern History*. New York: Penguin.

———. 2002. "Eating America." In C. Counihan, ed., *Food in the USA: A Reader*, 23–34. New York: Routledge.

———. 2008. "Food, Culture and Energy." In A. Nützenadel and F. Trentmann, eds., *Food and Globalization: Consumption, Markets and Politics in the Modern World*, 21–35. Oxford: Berg.

Moon, Okpyo. 2010. "Dining Elegance and Authenticity: Archaeology of Royal Court Cuisine in Korea." *Korea Journal* 50 (1): 36–59.

Morago, Greg. 2008. "Food Trends 2009: A Simply Happy New Year." *Houston Chronicle*, December 18, 2008. Online: http://www.chron.com/life/food/article/Food-trends-2009-A-simply-happy-new-year-1633144.php (accessed February 23, 2012).

Morgan, TaNoah. 2002. "Tackling Demands of New Languages: As Howard's Asian and Hispanic Populations Burgeon, So Do Courses in English and Spanish." *Baltimore Sun*, March 18, 2002. Online: http://articles.baltimoresun.com/2002–03–18/news/0203180198_1_korean-community-esl-courses-english (accessed March 1, 2012).

Morita, Yoshio. 1996. *Sūjiga kataru zainichi kankoku chōsenjinno rekishi* [History of Koreans in Japan told by statistics]. Tokyo: Akashi shoten.

Nestle, Marion. 2007. *Food Politics: How the Food Industry Influences Nutrition and Health*. Berkeley: University of California Press.

Neufeld, Sara. 2003. "Forum Aims to Win Trust of Korean Community: Law Enforcement, Asians to Discuss Justice System." *Baltimore Sun,* May 17, 2003. Online: http://articles.baltimoresun.com/2003-05-17/news/0305170344_1_korean-community-korean-presbyterian-church-kim (accessed March 1, 2012).

"Noodles in the US." 2013. *Euromonitor International,* December 2013. Online: http://www.euromonitor.com/noodles-in-the-us/report (accessed September 2, 2014).

Nützenadel, Alexander, and Frank Trentmann. 2008. "Introduction: Mapping Food and Globalization." In A. Nützenadel and F. Trentmann, eds., *Food and Globalization: Consumption, Markets and Politics in the Modern World,* 1–18. Oxford: Berg.

Odo, Franklin. 2004. *No Sword to Bury: Japanese Americans in Hawai'i during World War II.* Philadelphia: Temple University Press.

Office of Asian and Pacific Islander Affairs, State of Iowa. 2010. *Asian/Pacific Americans in Iowa: 2010.* Online: http://www.iowacapi.org/fileblob.asp?I=5443&table=content&ext=pdf&name=Asian-Pacific American in Iowa 2010.pdf (accessed April 28, 2012).

Office of the Registrar, University of Iowa. 2011. *A Profile of Students Enrolled at the University of Iowa: Fall Semester 2011.* Online: http://www.registrar.uiowa.edu/LinkClick.aspx?fileticket=NwxTwYUA0gc%3d&tabid=133&mid=579 (accessed April 6, 2012).

———. 2012. *Fall 2011 and Spring 2012 Tuition and Mandatory Fee Table.* Online: http://www.registrar.uiowa.edu/LinkClick.aspx?fileticket=%2fXgw5LMbt%2bM%3d&tabid=95 (accessed April 6, 2012).

O'Grady, Caitlin. 2003. "Care Line Helps Bridge Culture Gap for Korean Immigrants in Howard." *Baltimore Sun,* December 9, 2003. Online: http://articles.baltimoresun.com/2003-12-09/news/0312090392_1_korean-american-community-care-line-health-care (accessed March 1, 2012).

Oh, Tae-jin. 2010. "Why N. Korea Values Its Restaurants Abroad." *The Chosun Ilbo,* December 15, 2010. Online: http://english.chosun.com/site/data/html_dir/2010/12/15/2010121501157.html (accessed February 16, 2012).

Olesker, Michael. 1995. "Avoiding Clichés of Race, Crime in Weighing Verdict." *Baltimore Sun,* August 1, 1995. Online: http://articles.baltimoresun.com/1995-08-01/news/1995213042_1_joel-lee-black-korean-community (accessed March 1, 2012).

———. 1997. "City's Koreans in the Land of the Free, Home of the Slain." *Baltimore Sun,* January 30, 1997. Online: http://articles.baltimoresun.com/1997-01-30/news/1997030106_1_joel-lee-korean-community-park-heights (accessed March 1, 2012).

Organization for Economic Co-operation and Development (OECD). 2012. "Economic Survey of Korea 2012." In *OECD: Better Policies for Better Lives.* Online: www.oecd.org/korea/economicsurveyofkorea2012.htm (accessed December 1, 2013).

Paarlberg, Robert. 2009. *Starved for Science: How Biotechnology Is Being Kept Out of Africa.* Cambridge, MA: Harvard University Press.

Painter, Amelia. 2008. *Discover Iowa: Cooking with Iowa Wines, Meats, and Other Iowa Products.* Spencer, IA: Iowa Bed & Breakfast Innkeepers Association.

Pak, Jae-eun. 2006. *Yukkam yuhok: Geulsseuneun yorisa Pak Jae-eunui gamseong resipi* [Carnal sense, temptation: Emotional recipes of Pak Jae-eun, a chef who writes]. Seoul: Haenaem.

Park, Hye-Kyung. 2008. "Nutrition Policy in South Korea." *Asia Pacific Journal of Clinical Nutrition* 2008 (S1): 343–345.

Park, Jeanne. 2010. "South Korea in Ferment over Kimchi Shortage." *Need to Know on PBS,* October 5, 2010. http://www.pbs.org/wnet/need-to-know/the-daily-need/south -korea-in-ferment-over-kimchi-shortage/4087/ (accessed February 25, 2012).

Park, Madison. 2007. "Festival Keeps an Eye on the Future: Korean Community Celebrates Its Heritage and Passes It on to the Next Generation." *Baltimore Sun,* September 23, 2007. Online: http://articles.baltimoresun.com/2007-09-23/news /0709230041_1_korean-community-korean-festival-korean-culture (accessed March 1, 2012).

Park, Sungwoo. 2012. "Corn Imports by Korea to Rebound in 2012 as Hog Herd Builds." *Bloomberg Businessweek,* February 21, 2012. Online: http://www.businessweek.com /news/2012-02-21/corn-imports-by-korea-to-rebound-in-2012-as-hog-herd-builds .html (accessed April 27, 2012).

Patterson, Wayne. 2000. *The Ilse: First-Generation Korean Immigrants in Hawai'i, 1903–1973.* Honolulu: University of Hawai'i Press.

Pérez, Ramona Lee, and Meredith E. Abarca. 2007. "*Cocinas Públicas:* Food and Border Consciousness in Greater Mexico." *Food and Foodways* 15 (3): 137–151.

"Pyongyang Okryugwan naengmyeon matsseuro tteooreun songsan naengmyeon." 2005. *Choson.com,* June 9, 2005. Online: http://www.chosun.com/politics/news /200506/200506090260.html (accessed February 2012).

Robin, Marie-Monique. 2008. *The World according to Monsanto.* Film. DVD.

Ryang, Sonia. 1997. *North Koreans in Japan: Language, Ideology, and Identity.* Boulder, CO: Westview Press.

———. 2008. *Writing Selves in Diaspora: Ethnography of Autobiographics of Korean Women in Japan and the United States.* Lanham, MD: Lexington Books.

———. 2010. "To Be or Not to Be—In Japan and Beyond: Summing Up and Sizing Down Koreans in Japan." *Asia Pacific World* 1 (2): 7–31.

———. 2012. *Reading North Korea: An Ethnological Inquiry.* Cambridge, MA: Harvard Asia Center/Harvard University Press.

Schwabe, Calvin. 1979. *Unmentionable Cuisine.* Charlottesville: University of Virginia Press.

Schwieder, Dorothy. N.d. *Iowa Official History: History of Iowa.* Online: http://publi cations.iowa.gov/135/1/history/7-1.html (accessed April 5, 2012).

"Seoul Branch of Okryu Restaurant." 1999. *Korean Central News Agency,* June 11, 1999. Online: http://www.kcna.co.jp/item/1999/9906/news06/11.htm (accessed February 16, 2012).

Shi, Zumin, Natalie D. Luscombe-Marsh, Gary A. Yuan, Baojun Wittert, Yue Dai, Xiaoqun Pan, and Anne W. Taylor. 2010. "Monosodium Glutamate Is Not Associated with Obesity or a Greater Prevalence of Weight Gain over 5 Years: Findings from the Jiangsu Nutrition Study of Chinese Adults." *British Journal of Nutrition* 104: 457–463.

Shimogawa, Duane. 2013a. "Saks Fifth Avenue to Open First Hawaii Store in Waikiki." *Pacific Business News,* June 14, 2013. Online: http://www.bizjournals.com/pacific /news/2013/06/14/saks-fifth-avenue-to-open-first-hawaii.html (accessed December 25, 2013).

————. 2013b. "International Market Place Tenants in Waikiki Told to Leave by New Year's Eve." *Pacific Business News,* August 14, 2013. Online: http://www.bizjournals .com/pacific/news/2013/08/14/international-market-place-tenants-in.html (accessed December 25, 2013).

————. 2013c. "Developer Taubman Signs $87 M Lease for Waikiki's International Market Place Project." *Pacific Business News,* November 22, 2013. Online: http://www .bizjournals.com/pacific/news/2013/11/22/developer-taubman-signs-87m-lease-for .html (accessed December 25, 2013).

Siler, Julia Flynn. 2012. *Lost Kingdom: Hawaii's Last Queen, the Sugar Kings, and America's First Imperial Adventure.* New York: Atlantic Monthly Press.

"S. Korea Becomes World's Third Largest U.S. Beef Importer." 2010. *People's Daily Online,* July 16, 2010. Online: http://english.peopledaily.com.cn/90001/90777/90851 /7068926.html (accessed April 27, 2012).

"S Korea Dog Meat Row Deepens." 2001. *BBC News,* November 12, 2001. Online: http:// news.bbc.co.uk/2/hi/asia-pacific/1651543.stm (accessed March 29, 2012).

SNAP Monthly Data. 2013. "Supplemental Nutrition Assistance Program," November 8, 2013. Online: www.fns.usda.gov/34snapmonthly.htm (accessed December 1, 2013).

Song, Jason. 2002. "Sharing Aspects of a Rich Culture: Howard County's Growing Korean-American Community Works to Increase Its Visibility." *Baltimore Sun,* April 28, 2002. Online: http://articles.baltimoresun.com/2002-04-28/news/0204280248_1_ korean-american-community-korean-american-howard-county (accessed March 1, 2012).

————. 2003. "Videotapes Filling TV Void in Local Korean Community: Without Basic-Cable Outlet, Rentals Offer Soaps, Options." *Baltimore Sun,* March 9, 2003. Online http://articles.baltimoresun.com/2003-03-09/news/0303090272_1_korean-com munity-chong-rent-videos (accessed March 1, 2012).

Song, Young Jin. 2010. *The Korean Kitchen.* London: Southwater.

"South Korea Relaxes US Beef Ban." 2008. *BBC News,* April 18, 2008. Online: http:// news.bbc.co.uk/2/hi/business/7353767.stm (accessed April 27, 2012).

"South Korean Retailer Reinstates US Beef after Mad Cow Case." 2012. *The Telegraph,* April 26, 2012. Online: http://www.telegraph.co.uk/news/worldnews/asia/south korea/9227704/South-Korean-retailer-reinstates-US-beef-after-mad-cow-case .html (accessed April 27, 2012).

State Data Center of Iowa and the Office of Asian and Pacific Islander Affairs. 2011. *Asian/Pacific Americans in Iowa: 2011.* Online: http://www.iowadatacenter.org/Pub lications/api2011.pdf (accessed April 5, 2012).

Takagi, Mariko. 1987. "Moral Education in Pre-war Japanese Language Schools in Hawaii." MA thesis. University of Hawai'i. 1987.

Tannahill, Reay. 1973. *Food in History.* New York: Three Rivers Press.

Taylor, Charles. 1991. *The Ethics of Authenticity.* Cambridge, MA: Harvard University Press.

Terrazas, Aaron. 2009. "Korean Immigrants in the United States." *Migration Information Source,* January 2009. Online: www.migrationinformation.org/usfocus/display -cfm?ID=716 (accessed December 1, 2013).

"Total U.S. Beef Exports 2000–2009." 2009. *Statistics Provided by U.S. Government and Compliled by USMEF.* Online: http://www.usmef.org/downloads/Beef_2000_to_2009.pdf (accessed April 27, 2012).

Trilling, Lionel. 1972. *Sincerity and Authenticity: The Charles Eliot Norton Lectures, 1969–1970.* Cambridge, MA: Harvard University Press.

"2011 Farmland Value Survey." 2012. *Ag Decision Maker* File C2–70, January 2012. Online: www.extension.iastate.edu/agdm (accessed April 27, 2012).

Undergraduate Admissions, University of Iowa. 2011. *International Student Profile.* Online: http://www.uiowa.edu/admissions/undergrad/whos-at-iowa/international.htm (accessed April 6, 2012).

———. 2012. *International Student Profile.* Online: http://www.uiowa.edu/admissions/undergrad/whos-at-iowa/international.htm (accessed December 1, 2013).

"U.S. Beef Popular Again." 2008. *Chosunilbo,* August 19, 2008. Online: http://web.archive.org/web/20080822074337/http://english.chosun.com/w21data/html/news/200808/200808190017.html (accessed April 27, 2012).

"U.S. Beef Pulled from South Korean Shelves after BSE Report." 2012. *The Associated Press,* April 25, 2012. Retieved from *IowaFarmerToday.* Online: http://www.iowafarmertoday.com/news/livestock/u-s-beef-pulled-from-south-korean-shelves-after-bse/article_d993f7ea-8ed9-11e1-9496-0019bb2963f4.html (accessed April 27, 2012).

U.S. Census Bureau. 2010a. "U.S. Census 2010 Data: Maryland." Online: http://www.uscensus2010data.com/24-maryland-census-2010-data (accessed March 6, 2010).

———. 2010b. "U.S. Census 2010 Data: Kailua CDP (Hawaii), Hawaii." Online: http://quickfacts.census.gov/qfd/states/15/1523000.html (accessed September 11, 2014).

———. 2012. "State and County Quickfacts: Maryland." Revised January 17, 2012. Online: http://quickfacts.census.gov/qfd/states/24000.html (accessed March 6, 2012).

Van Sant, John. 2000. *Pacific Pioneers: Japanese Journey to America and Hawaii, 1850–80.* Urbana: University of Illinois Press.

Vongerichten, Marja. 2011. *The Kimchi Chronicles: Korean Cooking for an American Kitchen.* Emmaus, PA: Rodale Books.

Watanabe, Fumio. 1992. *Soba* [Buckwheat]. Tokyo: Sakuhinsha.

Watson, James. 2005. "China's Big Mac Attack." In J. Watson and M. Caldwell, eds., *The Cultural Politics of Food and Eating: A Reader,* 70–79. New York: Blackwell.

Watson, James, and Melissa Caldwell, eds. 2005. *The Cultural Politics of Food and Eating: A Reader.* New York: Blackwell.

Wilk, Richard. 1999. "'Real Belizean Food': Building Local Identity in the Transnational Caribbean." *American Anthropologist* 101: 244–255.

Williams, John-John IV. 2007. "Quality Translates Well: Ellicott City Market Designed for Korean Community Attracts a Wider Following." *Baltimore Sun,* May 28, 2007. Online: http://articles.baltimoresun.com/keyword/korean-community (accessed March 1, 2012).

Yamaguchi, Shizuko, and Kumiko Ninomiya. 1998. "What Is Umami?" *Food Reviews International* 14 (2–3): 123–138.

Yamashita, Samuel Hideo. 2013. "The Significance of Hawai'i Regional Cuisine in Post-colonial Hawai'i." In Robert Ji-Song Ku, Martin F. Manalansan IV, and Anita Mannur, eds., *Eating Asian America*, 98–124. New York: New York University Press.

Yang, Ouk-da. 2006. "Balhaeui myeotgaji eumsikseupgwane daehayeo" [A study of the food custom of the Balhae people]. *Hanguk godaesa yeongu* 42: 5–375.

Yang, Young-Kyun. 2010. "Well-Being Discourse and Chinese Food in Korean Society." *Korea Journal* 50 (1): 85–109.

Yoon, Sook-ja. 2005. *Good Morning, Kimchi! Forty Different Kinds of Traditional and Fusion Kimchi Recipes*. Seoul: Hollym.

Yuh, Ji-Yeon. 2002. *Beyond the Shadow of Camptown: Korean Military Brides in America*. New York: New York University Press.

Index

About the Author

Sonia Ryang is T. T. and W. F. Chao Professor of Asian Studies and director of the T. T. and W. F. Chao Center for Asian Studies at Rice University. At the time of writing this book, she was a professor of anthropology and international studies and C. Maxwell and Elizabeth M. Stanley Family and Korea Foundation chair of Korean studies at the University of Iowa. She received her PhD in social anthropology from the University of Cambridge. Her previous publications include *Reading North Korea: An Ethnological Inquiry* (2012).

Production Notes for Ryang | *Eating Korean in America*

Jacket and cover design by Julie Matsuo-Chun

Composition by Westchester Publishing Services
    with display type in Baker Signet and text type in Minion

Printing and binding by Sheridan Books, Inc.

Printed on 55 lb. House White Hi-Bulk D37, 360 ppi.